Modern
Turkey Hunting

Modern
Turkey Hunting
James F. Brady

A thorough guide to the habits, habitat, and methods
of hunting America's largest game bird

Introduction by R. Wayne Bailey

CROWN PUBLISHERS, INC., NEW YORK

ACKNOWLEDGMENTS

With thanks and appreciation to R. Wayne Bailey, North Carolina Wildlife Resources Commission; Gerald Wunz, Pennsylvania Game Commission; and Fred Evans, New York Department of Environmental Conservation—all of whom contributed valuable technical information or photographs, and accompanied me during that most vital aspect of research—hunting the wild turkey.

To Robert H. Boyle for his encouragement and help in initiating the writing of this book. To Walt Lesser and Jack Cromer, West Virginia Department of Natural Resources, for their courtesy and help. To Ira S. Latimer, Jr., Director, West Virginia Department of Natural Resources, for his hospitality.

I am also indebted to the publishers of *The American Rifleman* and *Outdoor Sports Life* for permission to use material first published in their pages.

To *Meleagris gallopavo,* the American wild turkey, for the many tense and thrilling moments he has given me in the forests.

CONTENTS

INTRODUCTION

The wild turkey reached its nadir early in the twentieth century and most observers predicted its extinction. Thousands of hunters of fifty or more winters readily recall that in their youths they never expected to see a wild turkey, and thousands of the more fortunate who had seen or hunted the species were convinced they would never be able to do so again. Thankfully, due to slow but steady changes in human and ecological events combined with the budding and flowering of the science of wildlife management, thousands, even millions, of hunters now annually have the opportunity to stalk the nation's largest and most elusive upland game bird. As a result their lives are much richer than would otherwise be the case.

Human beings evolved over millions of years in direct dependence upon the land and the wild creatures that freely roamed it. Most young men of today grew up in urban environments and because they have not lived close to the land are less likely to be hunters than their ancestors. As a result their lives are, sadly and all too frequently, less natural, less vigorous, and less meaningful. The cyclic abundance of game, recurring natural phenomena, and the whole mysterious universe provided the background for the development of early man's religious beliefs. Hunting was once an intrinsic part of the religion of all men; even today a significant portion of our people live primarily to hunt and fish. Of these few are more devoted to their sport than turkey hunters. In the words of Pete Farrar, one of America's most skillful turkey hunters, "Turkey hunting isn't a sport; it's a religion." If this book helps anyone to "get religion," to be more appreciative of the land and its wildlife, particularly of its wild turkeys and the wild places they need for survival, it will have served its purpose.

Because we live in an unreal, unnatural world, sentiment against hunting is growing. The opposition seems to be unaware of the necessary brevity of life in wild animals; of the relation of habitats to population densities; of the lingering agonies of natural deaths as compared to the swift, clean kills of the gun; and of the good health of low populations and the sicknesses prevalent on crowded ranges. This book, by a hunter, is for hunters and those who desire to be hunters.

Most of the "old-time, full-time" hunters and backwoodsmen who lived in the golden days of pristine turkey abundance are no longer with us. Many who will now and in the future pursue this bird, especially those in areas that until recently provided no hunting opportunity, will find themselves in need of a whole bag of ideas and technical know-how in order to attain even small measures of success. This book represents such a "bag" and is therefore most timely and welcome. Though intended primarily for the hunter, it covers the high spots of the life history, ecology, and management of turkeys in a manner that will appeal to nature lovers, environmentalists, and those with general interests in the outdoors.

Locating prospective hunting territory, identifying tracks, droppings, scratchings, dust baths, and other lore—all fundamental in turkey hunting—are subjected to in-depth treatment in this volume. Important as those things are, they are only starters. Skill in "talking" with the birds, in selecting callers, guns, cartridges, equipment, and accessories are knowledgeably handled by an author widely known not only as a hunter, writer, and gun expert, but perhaps more importantly as a gentleman, scholar, and sportsman.

Unlike most game species, turkeys are providing recreational hunting at two periods in each year—fall and spring, each with its distinctive rewards and delights. Many hunters who have equally sampled both are at a loss to decide which they prefer. Is the most enjoyable season in the cool, bright days of autumn when the hickories, maples, and poplars splatter the hillsides and coves with golden hues and the raven's croak may be the outstanding avian voice of the day? Or is it in the mellow warmth of dawn in April or May when amid the jasmine or dogwood blossoms a thousand notes and songs elicit deep-seated, long-cherished memories and emotions? If he prefers one over the other, the nimrod now has a choice or, better, he can savor both and in the process sharpen his touch at hunting.

Probably no hunter will dispute that the wild turkey provides the greatest challenge to *consistent* success of any game bird in America. This volume will be very helpful to anyone striving to meet that challenge.

R. Wayne Bailey
Milton, North Carolina

Modern
Turkey Hunting

1

The Return of the Prodigal

IT WAS still dark with that inky blackness peculiar to a moonless night, as I climbed. I could still hear the faint roar of the spring-swollen river in the valley below me. Great glacial boulders and the gnarled trunks of trees appeared momentarily in the beam of my flashlight as I picked my way up the steep mountainside. To the east, the sky was losing some of its blackness as I reached the oak- and beech-crowned ridge top, pausing to catch my breath.

The morning wind had not yet risen, and the only sounds were the sleepy first notes of small birds and the steady *put!-put!-put!* of the dew dripping from the trees and striking the matted leaves on the ground. As I stood listening intently, I was startled by the thunderous gobble of a wild turkey greeting the dawn from his roost some two hundred yards below me on the east-facing slope.

My heart pounded as I made my way stealthily down the slope in the direction from which the gobbler had sounded his morning salute. I had advanced about one hundred yards when a second and third gobble—coming close together this time—froze me where I stood. As I watched and listened, I heard the sound of great wing beats and the rustling of branches as the turkey left his roost and came to earth.

Looking around me in the increasing light, I spotted a slight depression in the forest floor behind the roots of a fallen tree. I scuttled quickly into this natural blind and placed my shotgun between two of the forked roots; then I removed the lidded box-type turkey call from my jacket and dropped the camouflaged face mask into position.

The turkey gobbled once more, and stroking the well-chalked lid across the thin edge of the box, I answered with the staccato *keow-keow-keow,* which is the mating call of the hen turkey. *Gilobble-obble-obble! Gilobble-obble-obble!* The sound rang through the morning air as the gobbler answered my call. Three or four minutes passed, and I sounded the mating call again. *Keeeow-keow-keow-keow!* The answering gobble came from a point much closer to me now. With shaking hands, I put the call aside and picked up my shotgun.

A querulous gobble came from just below a slight rise in the ground about fifty yards to my front. No answering with the call now! The slightest false note or faintest movement would give the show away. Peering through the mesh of the face mask, I saw a slight movement, and as if he had materialized from the ground, there stood a magnificent wild turkey gobbler in full spring breeding color and plumage.

Moving his bright-blue head from side to side as he advanced, he sounded a series of sharp, inquisitive clucks as he tried to locate the hen who had called to him. When he had advanced to within about thirty yards from my hiding place, I put the shotgun sight just below his head and pressed the trigger. The heavy load of small shot found its mark and I jumped from my blind and ran to possess what to me and to many sportsmen is the greatest trophy available to North American hunters.

Experiences such as this are becoming the lifetime treasures of an ever-increasing number of sportsmen as this great bird of the woodlands increases in numbers and range.

The wild turkey, *Meleagris gallopavo,* is a truly American bird. No solid evidence exists of its occurrence in other than its original historic range—east of the Rocky Mountains in the United States and Mexico, and from southern Ontario south to Florida. Fossil turkey bones have been found dating as far back as the Upper Pliocene period. No newcomer to the scene is this magnificent game bird!

The turkey was an important item of diet to the woodland Indians of the eastern United States, and various implements, such as awls and spoons, were made from its bones. The sharp spurs of the turkey were used as arrow points, and arrows were fletched with turkey wing-quill feathers. Although the Indians of Virginia and North Carolina kept some domesticated turkeys, large-scale husbandry of this bird was carried on only by the Indians of the southwestern United States and Mexico.

When Cortes entered Mexico, he discovered the Aztecs raising turkeys on a large scale. Some of these domesticated birds were brought back to Europe and are the probable origin of the barnyard turkey, a far different bird from the true wild turkey.

With the settlement of the United States and the subsequent clearing of the land, which destroyed the turkey's forest habitat, turkeys disappeared from much of their original range. Heavy hunting at all seasons of the year contributed to their decline. As the tide of settlement moved outward from the frontiers, the wild turkey gave way before it. Small populations continued to exist in wild and seldom penetrated patches of wilderness, notably in Pennsylvania, West Virginia, South Carolina, and Florida, but for the vast majority of sportsmen, hunting the wild turkey was in the class of unattainable dreams. The only real turkey hunting available during this period was in the swamps and canebrakes of the Deep South.

Attempts to restore the turkey to some of its former range were made by individuals and some state game departments. For various reasons, most of these efforts failed. Stockings with domestic turkeys were abject failures. These birds could not survive at all in the wilds, and many of them promptly joined domestic flocks in the nearest farmyards. Efforts were made to repopulate with birds obtained by back-crossing wild stock with the domestic strain on the theory that the wild strain would pass on to their progeny the characteristics necessary for survival in the wilds.

These efforts produce birds with some of the characteristics of the true wild turkey, but these populations still do not possess enough of the wariness and wildness of the wild strain to ensure survival. Many of these hybrid birds retained the inclination to join domestic flocks, and those that remained in the wild showed little ability to reproduce and spread into adjacent country. Efforts to stock with birds of the true wild strain raised on game farms were equally unsuccessful. These birds showed small ability to maintain huntable levels of population and, as with the crossbreeds, very little inclination to wander into and repopulate nearby ranges.

Release of these game farm birds showed poor results, and very few

In parts of the South, deep swamps provide excellent habitat for wild turkeys, as in this area in North Carolina.

of these birds were ever harvested by hunters. I've had some experience with these half-wild birds from a release that was made in suitable habitat some ten miles from my home. Shortly after release, some of these birds were observed feeding along the margins of a busy highway and on the lawns of homes in the area. Small populations of these game farm birds remain in various areas not too far from the point of release. From conversations I've had with game management officials, the general opinion is that the elimination of these game farm birds would be of benefit to the true wild turkey. What these biologists fear is genetic damage to populations of the wild birds should breeding occur between the two strains. The resulting progeny would be poorer in those characteristics necessary to survival.

Just as prospects for the restoration of the wild turkey were looking rather dim, nature itself took its rather efficient hand in the matter. After farming had reached its peak—prior to the Civil War in New York—cultivated fields reverted to brushy woodlands. These brushy early-growth forests provided ideal habitat for the whitetail deer and a population explosion occurred in this species that is still evident. The ruffed grouse also found a happy home in the brushlands and on abandoned farms, and provided magnificent sport for the hunter.

As this natural progression of the woodlands continued, and the trees reached maturity, surviving populations of wild turkeys spread into adjacent territory almost as soon as it provided habitat to their liking. This natural progression from brushland to mature forest is sometimes referred to by wildlife managers as being from deer-grouse habitat to turkey-squirrel habitat. Experienced hunters know that the best hunting for deer and grouse is often found in brushy early-growth areas, while squirrels prefer the more open and mature woodlands. It is in this same type of open forest preferred by squirrels that the wild turkey is most at home. The more mature trees produce the nuts, fruits, and buds that make up a large part of the turkey's diet. They also provide the essential roosting trees required by turkeys.

As an example of the turkey's inclination to occupy territory favorable to him, soon after World War II wild turkeys from northwestern Pennsylvania had migrated into bordering parts of western New York wherever the forest had reached a suitable stage of maturity. This migration into suitable habitat was noted in other parts of the country where these same conditions existed, though the natural reoccupation of territory by turkeys was a rather slow process in many areas. Good habitat devoid of turkeys might be separated from ranges inhabited by

Prime turkey range in Tucker County, West Virginia. Notice the open character of this hardwood forest. Problem . . . How would the turkey hunter hide himself? *Photo by Wayne Bailey*

Good turkey range is characterized by open forests with sparse undergrowth, as in this area in western New York.

wild turkeys by vast distances. These conditions precluded easy migration by turkeys into the unoccupied territories.

Confronted by this problem, wildlife managers busied themselves in discovering ways to give the turkeys a helping hand. Various attempts at live trapping were made, with little success at first. Cage-type wire traps proved fairly successful in taking wild birds, and the release of turkeys so captured into suitable unoccupied territory showed excellent results. Finally, the use of the mortar-thrown net—originally developed to take waterfowl—proved to be the answer to trapping turkeys in good numbers, and the greatest and most successful wildlife restoration project in recent history was under way in earnest.

The sportsmen of America would do well to give thanks to the dedicated wildlife biologists and game managers who are responsible for this magnificent achievement. They have, with the financial support of the hunters of America, done immense work toward the restoration and protection of the lands, forests, water, and wildlife of the United States.

A mortar-thrown net spreads over a flock of wild turkeys. *Photo by R. Wayne Bailey*

These men have spent untold hours in broiling heat and deadening cold, crouched in blinds near baited fields and clearings where—hopefully—wild turkey flocks would come within range of their mortar-thrown nets. That many of these vigils were not in vain is evidenced by the rapid spread and rise in turkey populations nationwide. It has been my pleasure and good fortune to hunt and "talk turkey" by the hour with quite a few of these men in various states. From them I've learned more about the natural history and hunting of the wild turkey than I could possibly have learned alone.

As of this writing, huntable populations of wild turkeys are present in thirty-six of our fifty states, and only four states have no turkeys at all. Healthy and growing flocks have been established by live trapping and transplanting in areas where prior plantings of game farm stock were abject failures. As frosting on the cake, wild turkeys have been established and are doing well in regions where turkeys never before existed. This is particularly true in states west of the Rocky Mountains.

There is every indication that with proper management and additional research, this happy chain of events will continue. All that is required is hunter support for the efforts of the wildlife biologists, game managers, and state game department personnel who are concerned with the management of the wild turkey.

Use of the mortar-thrown net to take wild stock for transplanting to new areas was the great breakthrough in the restoration of the wild turkey. Note the two mortars on the right in this photo. *Photo Courtesy West Virginia Department of Natural Resources*

Banded turkey being released in West Virginia. Studies of the movements and harvest of these banded birds enables game management personnel to learn much regarding the well-being of wild turkey populations. *Photo Courtesy West Virginia Department of Natural Resources*

Hen and poults captured by mortar-thrown net in West Virginia. They will soon be on their way to establish wild turkeys in a region previously devoid of this great game species. *Photo Courtesy West Virginia Department of Natural Resources*

2

At Home
in the Wilds

THE WILD TURKEYS of North America and the domestic bird that
graces the tables of nonhunters and unsuccessful hunters alike are all
members of the same species, *Meleagris gallopavo.* There all similarity
ceases. True wild turkeys are found over a wide geographic area, and
show differences in color, size, and some behavior patterns, according
to the area in which they occur. Turkeys inhabiting the moist hardwood forests of the eastern parts of the country are darker in color
than the birds of the dryer west. As is true with deer, northern birds
average larger in size than those found in more southerly regions. Other
differences, not so easily discernible without close study and examination, divide the species into various races.

They are: *Meleagris gallopavo silvestris,* the eastern woodland turkey, the bird of the eastern United States except Florida; *M. g. osceola,*
the smaller Florida turkey; *M. g. merriami,* the Rocky Mountain turkey; *M. g. intermedia,* the Rio Grande turkey; *M. g. mexicana,* inhabiting northwestern Mexico; and *M. g. gallopavo,* occurring in southern
Mexico, and the bird from which the name of the entire species is derived. Where the ranges of the different races overlap, turkeys will be
found that are intermediate in characteristics between the two races.

Note the worn and frayed tips of the primary wing feathers on this gobbler. This condition was caused by the wings dragging on the ground as the gobbler strutted. *Photo by Wayne Bailey*

The domestic turkey is probably a descendant of *Meleagris gallopavo gallopavo,* since this race occurs in the region once inhabited by the Aztecs. It is estimated that the turkey population of the United States at this writing is approximately 1½ million birds. Regardless of the subspecies found in any given area, sportsmen agree that with the return of the true wild turkey to much of his ancestral home, a new and stimulating challenge has arrived to test the hunter's mettle.

As the hours of daylight increase with the coming of spring, the wild turkey is caught up in the great plan and goal of life—the perpetuation of the species. Unlike most birds and mammals, female turkeys usually go to the males for mating when his majesty gives forth with the mating call that gives him his common name, "gobbler." It is frequently sounded at dawn, just before the gobbler descends from his roost, but is more often voiced after he has left the roosting tree and is on the ground.

Turkeys are polygamous and gobblers usually mate with several hens, which form his harem. In addition, he is ever ready to mate with any transient hen who succumbs to his wiles—providing his virility is up to the task. Since his recuperative powers are excellent, he is ready to perform again within a short time after mating. Gobblers will answer the mating call of the hen by gobbling in response to it. Emulating Mohammed, if the hen does not come to him, he will seek out the hen. This behavior of the gobbler is of extreme importance to the spring gobbler hunter and will be discussed in detail in the chapter on turkey calling. The whole technique of the spring hunt depends upon it.

When hens are in his presence during the mating season, the gobbler "struts" by erecting his tail in the shape of an immense fan and fluffing out his feathers to give the impression that he is larger than he actually is. The wing tips are dropped to the ground and the head and neck are drawn back tightly, assuming the form of the figure S. The gobbler pivots before the hen, displaying all his masculine splendor and frequently making a booming sound from deep within his chest. I've seen gobblers put on this display when coming to my call in the springtime. There is no more thrilling sight in nature than this love dance of the male turkey.

When their mating duties are over for the year, adult gobblers separate from the hens, not to be found in their presence again until the following spring. After mating and fertilization of the eggs, the hens seek out nesting sites in areas of low, brushy growth, with openings and edge nearby. Egg laying is irregular at first, but soon settles down

After mating, the hen turkey seeks out a spot in low, brushy growth to make her nest. *Photo by Nick Drahos, New York Conservation Department*

to a routine of one egg a day. When the full clutch is laid and incubation begins, the hen faithfully tends her nest, leaving it only for short periods in order to feed, dust, and water. Hatching occurs about twenty-eight days after incubation begins and the eggs usually all hatch within a period of twenty-four hours. If any of the chicks try to leave the nest before the hen wishes, she will push them back into the nest with her head and neck.

After the hen leads her brood away from the nest, the first few nights are spent on the ground, the chicks crouched under the hen's belly and wings. The chicks begin flying when they are about ten days old and are good flyers in eighteen days. When they are thirteen weeks old, turkey poults are two thirds the size of the mother hen, and at sixteen weeks the males have grown to be larger than their mother. With the approach of winter, these young males separate from the family flock and form all-male flocks of their own.

Male turkeys adhere to a rigid social order, segregated according to age class in their flocking. These flocks will consist of birds born in the spring of the year and recently separated from the family flock, birds approaching two years of age, three-year-olds, and the real-old settlers. The fabled "hermit gobblers" of many a stirring hunting story are probably the lone survivors of a flock of males that banded together some four or five years earlier. Each older age class will repel any attempts by younger birds to join their flocks.

Male turkeys usually do not breed until they are two years old, though at least in some areas, or in some years, they apparently do. On the other hand, yearling hens have been frequently observed with broods.

With the approach of the breeding season, male flocks break up into small groups. Often they will lay claim to a breeding territory and defend it as a team, repelling all invaders; the teams vary in size from two to five or more (sometimes larger where populations are high). Now gobbling begins in earnest. The gobbling is most intense just at break of day and tapers off at sunrise. This is the usual sequence, but I've heard gobbling as late as 11:00 A.M. Other hunters have told me of hearing intermittent gobbling all through the day. This late gobbling is probably by males who have not yet attracted a harem of hens. Gobbling will again be heard just before dark as the birds are ready to go to roost. This evening gobbling is probably a territorial announcement, a sort of "I don't want to find any of you guys around here in the morning!"

The feeding habits and diet of the wild turkey have been the sub-jects of intense study and research by wildlife biologists, and should be of equal interest to the turkey hunter. On his knowledge of how, where, and upon what turkeys feed will depend to a large extent his success.

The usual method of feeding by turkeys during late fall, winter, and early spring is by scratching. Leaves and other ground debris will be scratched away by the turkey's feet so as to expose whatever food items are available. When feeding on acorns, beechnuts, and the like, the birds will pick up the food and eat it whole. In late spring young blades of grass and the leaves of weeds and other plants will be eaten. Turkeys are omnivorous, and will eat insects, spiders, snails, and other small invertebrates whenever the opportunity arises. During emergency periods, such as when unseasonal heavy snow covers the ground, tur-keys will "bud" like grouse, flying up into the trees and picking the tender leaf buds. Beech buds are a favorite food during these periods.

Turkeys usually do their heaviest feeding during two main periods, midmorning and midafternoon. After leaving the roost, the flock will assemble with much yelping and clucking to call all hands together. After arriving at the feeding grounds, they will feed until midday, loaf about until midafternoon when feeding is resumed, and continue to feed until late afternoon or early evening when they again go to roost. Observations have shown that a single flock will feed over an area of from three to eight thousand acres, with three thousand acres being about average. The turkeys cover a fairly regular circuit while feed-ing, taking several days to a week to cover their feeding area. They are in constant motion as they feed, and cover a large piece of territory each day. Though fairly regular and constant in covering their feeding circuit, this is no clockwork procedure. Many a hunter has tried to arrive at a certain point on a flock's feeding circuit where he had ob-served them to pass at a certain time of day, only to find that the flock had already passed through.

Turkeys are extremely alert when feeding, and are difficult to ap-proach closely. No individual acts as a sentinel bird in a turkey flock, but each bird follows a procedure of scratch, listen, feed, look, scratch, look, feed, listen, all through the feeding period. Very few turkeys are killed by hunters stalking a feeding flock! Gobblers feed but little dur-ing the mating season, subsisting largely on the breast sponge, a layer of oily, spongy fat that lies over the breast. In early spring the breast sponge may make up as much as 11 percent of a gobbler's dressed weight. By early summer an active breeding gobbler will have used up

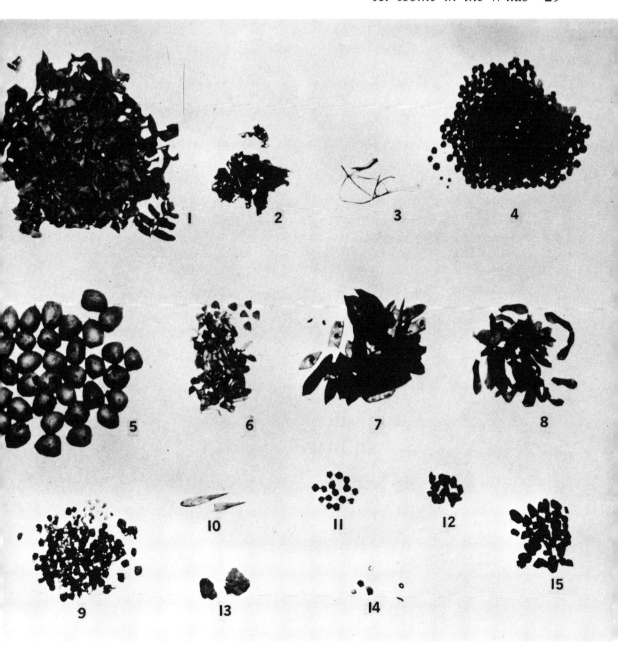

Some preferred turkey foods from the crop of a bird taken in Pocahontas County, West Virginia. 1. fern 2. fern 3. grasses 4. greenbrier 5. red oak 6. pipe vine 7. locust 8. maple 9. grape 10. ash 11. viburnum 12. ? 13. ground ivy 14. animal matter 15. grit. *Photo by Walt Lesser and Kermit Rinell*

this fat reservoir and his total weight will be much less than it was at the beginning of the breeding season.

During periods of heavy snow, turkeys may remain in trees for several days, all travel occurring by flying from tree to tree. After a heavy snowstorm in Virginia, which laid twenty-two inches on the ground, turkeys remained in trees from six to ten days. At such times turkeys will frequently feed at spring seeps, garnering such small insect and animal life as may be found there. The melted snow around these springs exposes tubers, roots, seeds, acorns, and other vegetable matter on which turkeys can feed. The turkey is a tough and hardy bird and can subsist and survive under conditions that would decimate a less resourceful species.

A great many birds and animals are known to prey upon the wild turkey, but such predation seems to have little effect on total turkey populations. The majority of professional wildlife managers are of the opinion that predation benefits total turkey populations by removing diseased and weakened birds. They recommend predator control only under specific and unusual conditions. The most severe losses from predation probably occur to nesting hens and their eggs, and to young poults just after leaving the nest and before they can fly. The turkey is a courageous bird and has been known to advance in a threatening manner upon a fox that disturbed its feeding. They have been known to attack dogs and even humans when they thought they were threatened, and turkey hens have been known to become airborne in pursuit of crows molesting their poults. In Pennsylvania a turkey hen was seen to attack a blacksnake that was carrying off one of her chicks in its mouth.

There is no doubt that turkeys can take care of themselves in the wilds. This fact has been thoroughly and painfully demonstrated to me on many occasions while hunting them. In the following chapters I'll set forth what I have learned from some of the finest turkey hunters in the country—and from that greatest teacher of all, the wild turkey.

During severe winters when deep snow covers their usual sources
of food, the resourceful wild turkeys will feed at spring seeps
such as this, where they will garner seeds, sprouts, tubers and
other vegetable matter, and small invertebrates such as snails,
worms, and insect life. *Photo by Wayne Bailey*

Although the wild turkey spends most of its time on the ground and will usually escape danger by running, it has excellent powers of flight that will be used to good advantage whenever the necessity arises. There are two turkeys in this picture, one of which is hidden by the bird in the foreground—or foreair. *Photo Courtesy North Carolina Wildlife Resources Commission*

3

Locating
Turkeys

THERE'S AN OLD SAW to the effect that "Before you can eat your fish you must catch it." To which might well be added, "Before you can catch your fish, you must fish where the fish are." This observation applies to turkey hunting in full measure. Very few turkeys will be taken by the hunter who blindly tramps through any woodlands reputed to harbor these birds.

As of this writing the only states with no open season for turkeys are as follows: Maine, New Hampshire, Massachusetts, Connecticut, Rhode Island, New Jersey, Delaware, Indiana, Minnesota, Iowa, Kansas, Nevada, Alaska, and Hawaii. Turkey populations are expanding so rapidly that before this sees print open seasons may be declared in some of these states. Illinois held its first open season in the spring of 1972; eighty-two turkeys were taken. Even far-off Hawaii reports good populations in small pockets. Meanwhile, with the exception of those living in Alaska and Hawaii, turkey hunting is available to all within a day's drive of home. Even those hunters living in the concrete desert of New York City need only drive two hours northward to the Catskill Mountains to find spring hunting for this magnificent game bird.

Probably the best bet for locating turkey-hunting areas is to contact the various state wildlife agencies. These agencies are supported by the sportsman's money and, in my experience, will invariably go all out in pointing the hunter in the right direction. Once the general turkey ranges within a state are located, the local agency personnel in these areas can usually furnish more explicit information as to where turkeys are ranging.

The wild turkey is a wide-ranging bird, and even when good, solid information has been received regarding general hunting areas, it's up to the hunter himself to pinpoint the location of turkeys on his proposed hunting grounds. It will pay the turkey hunter to be in the area to be hunted for several days before the season opens. If this is not possible, try to be on hand at least one day before the opening.

In the spring turkeys are likely to be in timber with brushy openings and edge nearby. These brushy areas provide the hens with good nesting sites. While they are incubating, hens will leave the nest several times during the day to feed, dust, and water. Other turkeys will also use these dusting spots, and they are one of the best indications that turkeys are ranging in a given area. Dusting by turkeys is done mostly in spring and summer, but may occur at other seasons if the weather is warm and the ground dry. It is such a fixed behavior pattern that turkeys have been trapped in West Virginia by loosening the soil and preparing ready-made dusting spots for them. A cannon trap-net was set after turkeys began using the dust bath. Their attention was fixed upon the dust bath as strongly as it would have been upon bait. These dust baths are easily recognized. They are shallow, oval-shaped depressions in dry or sandy soils, approximately two feet in length and about one foot wide. Loose turkey-body feathers are frequently found in them and in their vicinity.

Look for these dust baths, and for feathers, droppings, and turkey tracks in moist ground. The appearance of the droppings of the wild turkey will tell the hunter more about his quarry than will the spoor of any other game. From them, it can be determined whether it was a gobbler or a hen that made the deposit. The droppings of the gobbler are straight for most of their length, with a definite finial hook or curve at the end. They roughly resemble the letter J. Hen droppings are deposited in a neat, flattened spiral. This evidence can be important in choosing the hunting territory during a "gobblers only" season. Attention should be given to the apparent age of turkey droppings in assessing the choice of hunting grounds, taking into account the effects of rain, snow, and the weather in general.

A sure sign that turkeys are using a specific area, dusting spots such as this will be found on dry, sandy, or loose soils. Loose turkey body feathers in these dust baths indicate recent use.

While they are feeding, turkeys will scratch the ground bare of leaves, twigs, and other debris in their efforts to uncover choice items of diet. In this they are much like domestic poultry but operate on a much grander scale. These scratchings are a sure indication to the hunter that turkeys *were* in the vicinity. The wise hunter is constantly on the alert for these signs. The least information they can impart is that he is definitely in turkey country. While scratching, turkeys throw leaves, pine needles, and other ground cover to the rear, and the scratchings are roughly triangular in shape, with the apex pointing in the direction of the flock's travel almost like a directional arrow.

If the scratchings have been made recently, this fact will be evident from the moist earth—the last item to be uncovered and thrown to the rear—lying on top of the leaves and other litter. The leaves piled to the rear of fresh scratchings will be of a slightly darker color, due to their moisture content, than that of leaves on undisturbed ground. Old

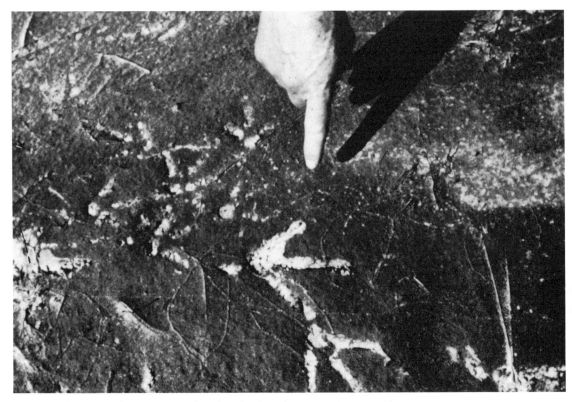

The turkey hunter must pinpoint the location of turkeys on his proposed hunting grounds. Look for tracks such as these around the edges of ponds and on moist ground.

scratchings will show dried earth and leaves matching their surroundings.

Hunters are sometimes puzzled as to whether the disturbed ground they come upon is the work of turkeys or of smaller birds, squirrels, or deer. The work of small birds and squirrels is of limited extent and haphazard, showing none of the definite directional characteristics of turkey workings. When feeding on mast, deer will sometimes tear up a good bit of territory in their line of travel. However, deer workings will usually cover a wider area and will be more rounded in shape than the typical triangular outline of turkey workings. Close examination will disclose deer tracks, and typical deer droppings will be found in the vicinity.

Droppings are not only a sign of the presence of turkeys in the area, but their configuration will indicate the sex of the birds. Upper left is a hen dropping. Note the hooked end of the gobbler dropping on the upper right. This sign of the gobbler is important to the spring hunter.

Turkey scratchings will show sharp toe marks like those made by a small rake or fork, and droppings will be characteristic of turkeys. In early fall when their food has not yet been covered by falling leaves, turkeys may do only intermittent scratching, but on the whole scratchings are of great importance to the hunter. When dry leaves cover the ground, a flock of turkeys will make a great racket by their scratching, and on a still day this sound can be heard from quite a distance. It resembles nothing so much as that made by an industrious householder raking the leaves on his lawn. An alert hunter hearing this sound can estimate the flock's line of travel and intercept them at a point that will give him a good chance for a shot.

Turkeys have loose feet and may wander over as much as a thousand acres a day in their traveling and feeding. Turkeys inhabiting mountainous areas are the greatest wanderers, and a flock may be at points many miles apart on successive days. Studies made in West Virginia showed that during the hunting season some flocks moved a maximum of fifteen miles. If all flocks moved such great distances, turkey hunting would be a will-o'-the-wisp affair, but fortunately, the average day's travel is two to four miles.

Most of the foregoing applies to fall and winter hunting for turkeys during which, in most states, turkeys of either sex may be taken. Hunting seasons held in the spring for gobblers only—which to me and a growing army of turkey hunters is the finest and most rewarding of all gunning sports—require the application of much that is contained in this chapter. There is, however, one ingredient present in the spring hunt that sets it above and apart from turkey hunting in general. This element of spring gobbler hunting will be dealt with in the next chapter.

Since the recent expansion of turkey populations all across the nation, and the ever-increasing opportunities to hunt this splendid game species, it would be a difficult task indeed to pinpoint any one particular area as offering the absolute optimum hunting.

In the Northeast, Pennsylvania and New York offer good turkey hunting, with Pennsylvania having much the larger population at this time. Turkeys in the Keystone State are well distributed, but the prime hunting areas lie in the north-central and northwestern counties.

New York's turkey population is growing at a great rate, helped by the trapping and transplant program carried on by the state. The best turkey hunting in New York as of this writing will be found in the southwestern part of the state, particularly in the counties of Cattaraugus, Allegheny, and Steuben.

Thanks to the efforts of the Division of Fish and Game, and to the sportsmen's financial support, which makes these efforts possible, the call of the wild turkey is again being heard in that mystic land of Rip Van Winkle, the Catskill Mountains. In the Catskill area, only Delaware County at present offers fall turkey hunting. In Sullivan and Ulster counties, spring hunting for gobblers only is permitted. As the turkey population of this area grows, fall hunting in all the Catskill counties will be available if, in the judgment of Fish and Game personnel, turkey populations and hunting pressure warrant it.

I can think of no finer way to spend a day in the springtime than to prowl a Catskill ridge in the forenoon, and then to spend the balance of the day casting a searching fly for trout over the fabled waters of the

Turkeys do most of their feeding on the ground, taking a wide variety of vegetable and insect matter. *Photo by Charles D. Peterson*

Beaverkill, the Neversink, the Willowemoc, or the Schoharie. That would surely be the best of all possible worlds.

Moving southward, Virginia and West Virginia have much to offer the turkey hunter. In Virginia the George Washington National Forest, lying along the border of West Virginia, is prime turkey country, as is the Blue Ridge Mountain region to the east across the valley of the Shenandoah. The Piedmont region of Virginia has good turkey hunting in certain areas.

The wild turkey was never entirely extirpated in the rugged mountain country of West Virginia, although populations were reduced to the point where grave concern was felt for its future. Protective laws and a vigorous program of trapping and transplanting wild stock carried on by the Department of Natural Resources have assured fine hunting for this species in the Mountain State.

The best turkey ranges in West Virginia lie in the eastern part of the state in the Allegheny Mountain region and in the Eastern Panhandle. In the Panhandle region the counties of Grant, Hardy, and Pendleton are excellent turkey areas. In the eastern mountain region of the state, Greenbrier, Pocahontas, and Randolph counties usually lead in the total take of wild turkeys, with Webster and Tucker counties right behind them. Most of the best turkey range in this region is in the Monongahela National Forest, which covers some 800,000 acres. West Virginia is one of my favorite hunting grounds.

North Carolina is conducting an intensive wild turkey restoration project under the able leadership of Wayne Bailey. There is little—if anything—that Wayne doesn't know regarding the management of this species at the present level of available knowledge. He is in all likelihood the world's leading authority on the subject, and anyone who has had the privilege of hunting turkeys with Wayne can count himself as being fortunate indeed.

The coastal plain and Piedmont sections of North Carolina offer good turkey hunting, and the transplanting of stock to the western mountainous region of the state, where excellent habitat exists, is building up a fine population of turkeys in this rugged area. The future looks bright for turkey hunting in North Carolina.

My turkey-hunting experience has been in the states just mentioned. When we've found something good fairly close to home we tend to stick with it. Information gathered from various sources indicates the following as being what can be expected in other states having open seasons at this time. These seasons vary as to type with the individual states, and are of four classifications. These are: fall hunting for either sex; spring hunting when gobblers only may be taken; fall hunting for gobblers only; and spring hunting for gobblers only, followed by fall hunting for either sex.

Some may take exception to this listing, asserting that turkey hunting in some particular state is much better than is indicated. Those who do so will be experienced turkey hunters who know their local hunting territories well, and who keep an eye out for turkey movements and signs throughout the year. For these very reasons they are highly successful in taking turkeys.

Satisfaction with the results of a morning's gobbler hunt in West Virginia is apparent in these smiling faces.

The listing is based on reports of turkey populations in each state listed and, in some instances, on turkey harvest reports by state agencies. With the rapid increase in turkey populations, the picture can change radically over a very short period of time. This is a development of which I heartily approve.

Alabama — Excellent
Arizona — Good
Arkansas — Good
California — Fair
Colorado — Good
Florida — Excellent
Georgia — Good
Idaho — Spotty
Kentucky — Spotty
Louisiana — Fair
Maryland — Spotty
Michigan — Fair
Mississippi — Excellent
Missouri — Excellent
Montana — Fair
Nebraska — Spotty
New Mexico — Good
North Dakota — Fair
Ohio — Spotty
Oklahoma — Good
Oregon — Fair
South Carolina — Good
South Dakota — Good
Tennessee — Good
Texas — Excellent
Utah — Fair
Washington — Spotty
Wyoming — Fair

Bag limits vary from state to state. Most states having a spring gobbler and a fall either-sex season allow the hunter to take one gobbler in the spring and either a hen or gobbler in the fall. Other states have higher annual and/or season limits. Since bag limits may change from year to year, the current laws for your intended hunting area should be checked.

Turkey hunter's camp in North Carolina. *From left to right:*
Jerry Wunz, biologist with the Pennsylvania Game Commission;
Wayne Bailey, leader of North Carolina's Wild Turkey Restoration Project; Frank Piper, President of Penn's Woods Products,
manufacturer of turkey calls. Author is behind the camera.

4

Hunting the Spring Gobbler

THE THOUGHT of hunting any game in the springtime is at variance with all the concepts, customs, conventions, and traditions of generations of sportsmen. So much so that on some occasions when I've broached the subject of spring turkey hunting to those not familiar with the sport, my listeners gave every indication of regarding me as a poacher, game hog, and altogether reprehensible character, probably given to dynamiting trout pools, jacklighting deer, and shooting ducks on the water.

This attitude is understandable. Hunting seasons are traditionally held in the fall and winter when most species of wildlife have concluded their breeding activities and their young have been raised. Game populations are high and the harvest can begin. All very logical and sound reasoning. It may seem strange, therefore, to state that the spring hunting of turkey gobblers is, biologically, a more sound procedure in regard to its effect on total turkey populations than is the hunting of turkeys in the fall when any turkey is fair game.

Biologists who have specialized in the study and management of the wild turkey are practically unanimous in stating that spring hunting is to be preferred where new populations have been established or where restoration of a low population is the goal. Their conclusions on the subject can be summed up as follows.

(1) The procedure in spring hunting is to call up a gobbling bird. Therefore, only males are harvested. Since turkeys are polygamous, most males are in excess of reproductive needs, and their removal has no relation to total populations in the following year.

(2) Removal of a portion of the males may improve reproduction by reducing their interference with nesting hens. Some are of the opinion that male turkeys are more likely to cause this "interference" than are hunters. Most states require hunters to stop their activities sometime in the forenoon in order to obviate any possible disturbance that might cause hens to abandon their nests.

(3) Spring seasons are set so that hunting begins after the peak of mating has passed. Therefore, spring hunting does not interfere with reproduction. Sperm cells are known to live for as long as fifty-six days in the female reproductive tract.

(4) Many marginal turkey areas, in which turkeys could be practically wiped out in fall seasons, are entirely capable of providing quality spring hunting. Some states with high turkey populations traditionally hold spring seasons only.

To the turkey hunter spring is the finest time of all to be afield. This is the only time of the year when the turkey advertises his presence by gobbling. Spring gobblers are magnificent trophies, fat and colorful, and at their heaviest weights. The weather is usually—but not always— mild and zestful. Since most states require hunting to cease by noon at the latest, in areas where both occur, spring turkey hunting can be combined with trout fishing to make it a double-barreled sporting venture. Most fly hatches at this time—late April and early May—come off in the late morning and early afternoon and the turkey hunter-trout fisherman can sample the best of two splendid outdoor activities.

Preseason scouting of the hunting area is important in all turkey hunting, and is almost essential to success when hunting the spring gobbler. When the all-male flocks break up just prior to the spring mating season, each gobbler establishes his strutting and gobbling territory, defending it vigorously against intrusion by other males. Individual territories may be separated by fairly long distances, and the whole technique of spring hunting is based on locating individual gobbling birds. Turkeys are not to be found on every ridge, and it is up to the hunter to pinpoint the game.

Fortunately for the hunter, spring is the time when the gobbler cooperates by announcing his presence to all who will listen—and who know what to listen for. Locating gobblers in the springtime calls for early rising on the part of the hunter. Just at daybreak, gobblers still in their roosting trees will usually gobble several times before flying down to the ground. After leaving his roost, the gobbler will again send forth his lusty summons to his harem of hens. To my mind there is no more thrilling sound in the wilds than the thunderous gobble of the tom turkey in the springtime. It has given rise to his title of "Mountain Shaker" among those who pursue and love this great bird.

The location of gobbling turkeys prior to the opening of the season is in itself a great way to spend a fine spring morning. If a network of roads traverses the hunting territory, driving along and stopping every half mile or so to listen for gobbling will reveal the presence of many birds. Since each gobbler has staked out his territory, you can be almost certain that once a bird has revealed his presence by gobbling, he will be found in the same general area on subsequent mornings.

In roadless areas a morning's walk through the woods, again with stops to listen for gobbling birds, is a wonderful way to prepare yourself both mentally and physically for the coming hunt. Be alert on these scouting trips for other signs of turkeys such as dusting spots, tracks in moist ground, and especially the characteristic gobbler droppings. Above all listen very intently for the sound of gobbling.

What is it that we are listening for? Once heard, the gobble of the wild turkey will never be forgotten or mistaken for anything else. It is similar to the gobbling of the domestic tom, but is much finer and clearer in tone. At a distance it resembles the baying of a small hound with a voice of the type known as a "chop" among hound men.

On a clear morning gobbling can be heard for up to a mile, especially in mountainous country. As you travel through the proposed hunting territory prospecting for turkeys, at each stop if you hear no gobbling, use whatever calling device you favor to sound the mating yelp of the hen. Some turkeys may not gobble at all on a specific morning or may have gobbled before you arrived in the vicinity. When you send out the hen yelp from your call, they will usually answer with a gobble.

When you hear an experienced turkey hunter speak of "owling," he is referring to another technique that is sometimes effective in inducing a gobbler to sound off. Just at daybreak while the birds are still on the roost, if you can imitate the hoot of an owl, this sound is sometimes better for the purpose than the mating yelp of the hen turkey. In actual hunting owling is the better technique, as a gobbler on the roost will expect any hen he hears to come to him and he may stay on the roost for an hour or more if he hears what he presumes to be an anxious hen.

In late afternoon and early evening gobblers can be located by listening for the gobbles they sound after going to roost. These territorial announcements are made to warn away other gobblers and to let the hens know where their lord is roosting. At this time of day gobblers will frequently sound off when they hear any sharp noise. They will answer to such diverse sounds as the blast of an automobile horn, the sound of two boards being clapped together, and gunshots. One old hunter told me of locating gobblers in the evening by sounding a bugle. According to him, the penetrating blast of the brass horn "really set 'em to gobbling."

The use of a box call of the type known as a gobbling box to imitate the gobbling of the turkey will really pinpoint the location of roosting toms in the evening. It is my favorite way of setting up the next morning's hunt.

Try to put yourself in the roosting gobbler's frame of mind. He has laid claim to his breeding territory, and has gathered about him a harem of willing hens who look upon him as the lord of the mountain. He's had a fine day, gathering his harem early in the morning and breeding with each of them. He has succeeded in enticing that new young hen from over the ridge into his circle of concubines. The balance of this beautiful spring day has been spent in loafing about and patroling his bailiwick.

Now he has chosen a good roosting tree not too far from where his hens are roosting, and is settling down for the night in an altogether self-satisfied mood. Anticipating another glorious day tomorrow, he is preparing to sleep. Suddenly, his complacency is shattered by a raucous, challenging gobble from somewhere below him on his ridge! Almost as a reflex, he answers the interloper's challenge with a reverberating gobble of his own—and thereby gives away his location. You can be 99 percent certain that he will be right there or in the immediate vicinity on the following morning.

If at all possible, experienced turkey hunters will have several gobblers located before the opening of the season. The more the better, for any one gobbler may have been disturbed and have moved from his usual location. It just doesn't make sense to have the success of your hunt depend on having a fix on one turkey. Then, too, some other hunter may have located and be intent on bagging the same bird. Some of the greatest turkey-calling contests of all time have occurred when two good callers have vied with each other in trying to toll in the same gobbler! The hunter with the most calling tricks up his sleeve usually wins.

On the evening before the great day be sure to get a good and full night's rest. You'll be rising at an early hour. As my friend Frank Piper of Pennsylvania, turkey-call manufacturer and expert hunter, puts it, "A late start can kill you in this game." Most of the action in spring gobbler hunting takes place in the first hour after daybreak and it will pay you to be on the scene. The smart hunter will avoid drinking and a late bedtime when spring gobbler hunting is the game. Long before daylight you'll be in the woods, picking out the way to your chosen spot in the beam of your flashlight. Over a large part of the country you'll have a stiff climb before you. The well-rested and alert hunter is more likely to bring home his gobbler.

Getting into position well before daybreak is all-important to bringing home a gobbler that will "hang by his spurs." When you have a gobbler located, try to work your way to within about two hundred yards or slightly closer to his estimated position. Make as little disturbance as possible. You cannot move through the woods in darkness without making some noise, but slight sounds such as the breaking of twigs underfoot and the swishing of brush and branches disturbed by your passage are normal night sounds made by many nocturnal animals, and roosting turkeys will pay little heed to them.

The last hundred yards or so to the position you've selected should be traversed without the aid of your flashlight. You'll become adept at moving in total darkness after a few trials. Go slowly. You've given yourself more than enough time, so make use of it.

Once in position, there is nothing to do but wait. The good turkey hunter will have mastered the waiting game. Pull your collar up higher to ward off the slight night chill and—think turkey. Mull over in your mind all you've learned about turkey hunting. Silently rehearse the cadence and timing of the mating yelp of the turkey hen. Mentally picture your gobbler sitting in his roosting tree downslope from you. If you've done your homework properly—he is there!

As daybreak approaches, the twittering and calling of small birds begin. This is your signal to be on the alert. As the sky starts to lighten in the east, your gobbler may start to sound off while still on the roost. If he does not, and you can imitate the hoot of an owl, this may start him gobbling and pinpoint his location. If your "owling" sounds more like the croaking of an asthmatic frog, there is a commercial "Owl Hooter" on the market that is breath-operated and does a fair job of "owling."

Don't use your turkey call to make the mating yelp of the hen at this moment. Remember, the hens normally come to the gobbler for mating, and if you call while he is still on the roost, the gobbler may just stay there answering your hen yelps by gobbling in reply. Under these circumstances he may stay there for an hour or more—although this is exceptional—in expectation of sighting an approaching hen.

If the gobbler sounds off of his own volition or in answer to your owl hoots, be patient. Make no answering calls, either by owling or with your turkey call. Listen intently, more intently than you have ever done before. If it is a quiet morning, you will be able to hear the turkey leave his roost and alight on the ground. He will probably come to earth some sixty to eighty yards from his roosting tree, planing down to some small opening that is clear of brush and vines.

You can now understand why your approach to a roosting gobbler should be no closer than about 150 yards. Aside from the danger of the gobbler seeing you, if you have approached nearer than this and should his descent from the roost be in your direction, you might well be wearing a twenty-pound wild turkey gobbler as a headpiece. Such an event is bound to fluster the calmest of hunters.

If you have heard the gobbler leave his tree, or if sufficient time has elapsed since daybreak so that he has in all probability flown down, be ready to call. Make a soft series of three or four hen yelps starting with a slightly drawn-out quaver and ending with the yelps. *Keeeow-keow-keow.* Do not call loudly at this juncture—the gobbler has keen hearing and will easily hear your soft yelping.

Nine times out of ten, your call will be answered by a booming gobble. Here again, patience will pay off. Do not come right back with an answering hen yelp. You and the gobbler are now fully engaged in a contest of wills. He, thinking you are a hen, will attempt to lure you to him by gobbling and strutting. You must play the role

Moving into a position about 200 yards from a roosting turkey at daybreak, the spring gobbler hunter sounds a series of soft hen yelps on his turkey call. If there is no answering gobble, he will wait five minutes or so and then sound another series, a little louder in volume.

of a turkey hen who is not overly impressed by his majesty's display of masculine vigor.

If the gobbler, in the parlance of turkey hunters, "hangs up" and does not advance toward you but continues to gobble, sound the mating yelp of the hen at intervals of five to seven minutes. If you cease calling altogether, as some advise, he may think the supposed hen has left the scene. A fine balance must be struck between too much and too little calling. Call just enough to keep him interested.

If the turkey stops gobbling, be alert, for he may be coming straight toward you or be circling your position preparatory to coming in from your side or rear. He may or may not gobble while making this circling movement.

When hunting in hilly or mountainous country, if the turkey gobbles from a position to either side of and above you, move as quickly and silently as possible to a position at least fifty yards above him. For some unknown reason it is easier to lure a turkey uphill when calling.

With the gobbler advancing toward your position, make a last-minute check of your concealment and equipment. Raise your gun to a position where it can be brought to bear on the turkey with the least possible movement. More than one turkey has been spooked at the last moment by the morning sun reflected from a moving gun barrel. Make sure no item of equipment is placed where you might accidentally knock into it and cause a disturbing noise. This is the moment you have waited and planned for—make it good.

Turning your head slowly, you catch a slight movement to your right front through a screening of brush. Put your call aside now; its work is done. *Slowly* bring your shotgun to bear in the turkey's direction. Suddenly, he is there before you in full strut, his neck drawn back tightly against his chest, his tail feathers spread out in an enormous fan, and his wing tips dragging on the ground. As he continues to advance, you can see the beard dangling from his chest and are startled to hear the *vrooomm!* from deep within his chest as he sounds the typical "pulmonic puff" made by a strutting gobbler.

Now is the time when you must display the utmost discipline. You'll be tempted to shoot even though the gobbler is at least a full fifty yards from your hiding place. This is much too long a range at which to attempt the preferred and deadly head and neck shot. Keep tight control of yourself and wait until the turkey approaches to within twenty-five to thirty yards of you. Remember, this is an outside range of

Every sense alert and ready to depart at the slightest hunter error, a wild turkey gobbler approaches the source of a hunter's calls. This is the point at which many opportunities are lost by the hunter who cannot keep still or who waits until this moment to bring his gun into position for the shot. *Photo by Fred Evans*

ninety feet, and preferably the shot should be delivered when the bird is somewhat closer.

Your gun muzzle has been covering the gobbler all during his approach, and no sudden—and probably disastrous—gun movement is necessary. The wild turkey has far greater keenness of vision than man, and any slight movement now will set him instantly on the alert and diving for cover.

Well within range now, the gobbler ceases his strutting and clucks inquisitively as though to ask the hen "Where are you?" He moves his head from side to side and those bright piercing eyes seem to knife through all your attempts at concealment—revealing you for what you are. With shaking hands and pounding heart, you hold the front sight just below the junction of his bright blue head and neck and press the trigger. He is not yet yours. *Run* to where the gobbler is beating his great wings on the ground and take possession of him. Many hunters

The gobbler hunter's supreme moment. Convinced that the hunter's calls are those of a hen, His Majesty, now well within range, goes into full strut with his tail spread like an enormous fan, and his wing tips dragging on the ground to impress the hen with his masculine splendor. From the closeness of the range, the reason for the spring turkey hunter's preference for the shotgun is apparent. *Photo by Fred Evans*

have stood in open-mouthed consternation as the turkey they thought to be dead revived and ran off mortally wounded. Such a bird will most likely hide in some hollow stump, downed treetop, or rocky and brush-screened crevice where it will eventually die. You've worked too hard and planned too long to let a moment's lapse rob you of your trophy. Hold up your gobbler by his feet and admire his beauty as the sun glints from his bronzed and shining plumage. In your hand you hold your diploma as a turkey hunter.

The scene unfolds in just such fashion each spring, and it is my fond wish that your first turkey hunt should end in just this way. That not all hunts do can be attested to by every hunter who has passed through the primary grades in the school of turkey hunting.

Many things can change the picture.

Your gobbler may not cooperate in coming to you because his harem of hens is nearby, and he is busily mating with them and not inclined to succumb to the flirtatious yelping of some transient hen. All is not lost under such circumstances, for rest assured he has heard your

After the shot, the smart hunter gets to his downed bird immediately. Too many hunters have watched a supposedly dead
turkey revive and take off for parts unknown through failure
to observe this caution.

calling and after attending to his procreative duties and enough time has elapsed so that his vigor has been restored, his vanity will impel him to seek out any other willing hen.

Under such circumstances the hunter should make with his call a series of hen yelps every fifteen minutes or so. This will let the gobbler know that the strange hen he has heard calling is still interested and in the vicinity. Here again, patience will pay off and an hour is not too long to spend when you know that you are in an area used by a particular gobbler as his mating and strutting ground.

Be on your guard. A gobbler will many times approach your position silently with never a gobble and from any direction. A favorite trick of wise old gobblers is to circle the source of the calling and approach from the rear. This has happened to me on more than one occasion, and the turkey has usually managed to escape when I finally became aware of his presence and attempted to swing around in my hidey-hole and bring my gun to bear. The hunter's best bet when a bird approaches from behind is to jump quickly to his feet—which will cause the turkey to freeze momentarily and allow time for the gun to be leveled and the shot taken. I'm sure that many times a crafty gobbler has come up on my rear, assessed the situation, and silently disappeared without my ever knowing that he had been there. Be especially watchful for this maneuver whenever a turkey who has been gobbling in answer to your calling and has been coming in nicely suddenly stops gobbling as he draws nearer.

Sometimes the hunter, tiring of holding his gun, is tempted to place it on the ground or lean it against some object where it is just out of reach. Don't! During a recent spring season in West Virginia, I had been working on a reluctant gobbler with my call for the better part of an hour. I had located this bird by walking along a ridgetop and calling every three hundred yards or so. The turkey had answered my calling by gobbling from a point about two hundred yards down-slope from me. As we carried on our conversation, it seemed to me that he was making a circle to my left, which would bring him across the ridge and behind me. When he gobbled from a position directly to my left and still about two hundred yards distant, I changed position so as to face down the opposite slope and in the direction from which I expected him to approach.

The turkey continued to gobble in an effort to bring the supposed hen to him, and I played the waiting game by yelping occasionally in answer. I could tell from his gobbles that he was now on the side of the ridge below me in the new direction. He continued to gobble and I gave an occasional answering yelp. By now I had leaned my gun against a fallen tree to my left, having grown tired of carrying and holding it all morning, and the gobbler still being quite a ways off.

As I continued to peer intently in the direction from which I had heard the last gobble, I was startled to hear a loud *cluck!* off to my left side. Glancing in that direction, I was amazed to behold a gobbler standing not twenty yards from me. I dropped the call, reached for my gun, and leaped to my feet. Too late! This new gobbler was a mere dark streak arrowing through the brush; I saw my shot charge shredding the leaves on the ground a good three feet behind his tail.

Had I been holding my gun in readiness as I should have been, I would have collected my gobbler right then and there. Needless to say, the gobbler I had originally been working on silently departed the scene, not to be heard from again that morning. Even so, as the fellow is reputed to have said just before he was hung, "I wouldn't 'uv missed the experience for anything."

It will often happen that a gobbler will come in silently, as this bird did, when he has heard another gobbler answering to hen yelps. Probably just sneaking in with the idea of stealing the hen for himself. It pays to be alert and ready at all times when turkey hunting, particularly when hunting the gobbler in the springtime.

Calling up more than one gobbler is a fairly frequent occurrence in the turkey woods. A few seasons ago I was hunting spring gobblers in North Carolina with Wayne Bailey, Jerry Wunz, turkey biologist with the Pennsylvania Game Commission, Charley Peterson, wildlife manager, and Frank Piper, manufacturer of the Roger Latham calls. On the morning after I left to be in New York for the opening of the spring gobbler season, Charley called up five birds from one stand.

I had located the first gobbler on the West Virginia ridge in the incident just related, by walking through good turkey range as determined by tracks, droppings, dust baths, and good solid information. I had not been able to arrive in the area early enough to locate a gobbling bird in the morning or evening hours of the day prior to this hunt.

Under these conditions gobblers can be located by walking through good turkey country, starting just at daybreak, and listening for gobbling birds. If no turkeys are heard, stop every three hundred yards or so and call by sounding the hen yelp. Call softly at first; a gobbler may be only a short distance away. If no answering gobble is heard, increase the volume of your calling, listen intently, and be prepared to dive for cover!

I make it a practice to glance around me before calling under these circumstances in order to pick out a good hiding place in the event that a gobbler should answer from close by. At times a gobbler will answer and come in on the run. If you have not located a good place of concealment beforehand, he may be on top of you before you can gather your wits. If this should happen, your only alternative is to drop flat on the ground and make the best of an awkward situation. A little forethought will enable you to avoid this little comedy. Yes! It has happened to me!

Do not, when calling turkeys, attempt to hide yourself in dense brush. These wary birds will not approach thick cover, preferring to advance over and through fairly open ground. Find a position that will lightly screen you from those probing eyes. Root holes, fallen logs, and downed treetops are the sort of natural cover to use for concealment. Combined with a camouflage jacket, cap, gloves, and face mask, they will hide you well enough.

As the turkey approaches, in addition to having your gun in a ready position and pointed toward the area where you expect the turkey to appear, make sure the safety is off or the hammer cocked before the bird is in close. The loud metallic sounds made by operating the safeties or hammers on some guns will surely frighten off many birds that approach within decent shooting range. Most guns can be adjusted so that these mechanical sounds are kept to a minimum, and it is well worth the effort to do so. If the safety is off or the hammer cocked, and for some reason the shot is not taken, remember to move the safety to "on" or lower the hammer before moving from your position.

In many instances the sight of the gun barrel itself will spook a turkey that is coming in well to the call. Most gun barrels will reflect the low morning sun like a mirror. Even a small movement of an inch or so will send out a warning flash of light to the oncoming turkey. I am convinced that I've lost many opportunities to bag my gobbler from this cause alone.

Camouflaged from head to foot and well hidden, I've had gobblers go from full strut to full alert at the last moment when I—ever so slowly—moved the muzzle that last few inches that would bring it

Caught in the open by a gobbling tom at close range, this hunter
makes the best of it by dropping flat on the ground and using his
box call in answer to the gobbles.

to bear on my prospective gobbler. In order to keep this cause of
lost opportunities to a minimum, I make it a practice to avoid having
my gun barrel protrude more than a few inches from whatever cover
I am in.

I've also been experimenting with the use of camouflage tape of the
type used by archers to cover their bows. This tape comes in lengths
that are just about right for applying to gun barrels. Anything that
will serve to conceal the hunter and his equipment from this gimlet-
eyed bird will be of help.

Many a turkey has been spooked by the glint of morning sunlight from a shotgun barrel. Protruding from concealing cover, the barrel of this gun has been masked with camouflage tape in an effort to conceal it from old "gimlet-eyes."

Why confirmed turkey hunters keep coming back for more. Wayne Bailey holds a prime spring gobbler taken in Bath County, Virginia.

Turkeys should be field dressed immediately after they are taken. This is especially important during the periods of warm weather often encountered in the spring and early fall. While field dressing the bird, don't overlook the crop that may be filled with recently ingested food. Failure to take these precautions may result in the rapid spoilage and souring of what is considered by many to be the finest of all wild game for the table.

Any recipe for cooking the domestic bird may be used in preparing the wild turkey for the festive board. As in the cooking of all wild game birds, special efforts should be made to keep the meat moist. Don't forget the giblets for gravy. Highly seasoned sauces and dressings are considered necessary by many folks in preparing all wild game. In my opinion these concoctions serve only to mask the delicate flavors that should be savored as the rightful reward of the successful hunter.

If you are a fly-fisherman and tie your own flies, the wild turkey offers an additional bonanza. Feathers from the wild turkey's body, wings, and tail are used in tying a vast number of fly patterns for the taking of trout, salmon, and bass. Nonfishermen should save these feathers for fly-fishing friends who will appreciate the gift more than were it a bottle of "The Best." Since the feathers from the true wild turkey are comparatively rare, they might be sold to dealers in fly-tying materials. Check your state laws on this.

Hunting the gobbler in the springtime offers more pure enjoyment and sport than does fall hunting, when any turkey may be taken. For the new turkey hunter, spring turkey hunting is most likely to be crowned with success. Once he has brought one of these great trophies to bag and, holding it at arm's length, sees the morning sun reflected in hues of green, bronze, and purple from its magnificent plumage, he is a turkey hunter forever.

5

Fall Turkey Hunting

DESPITE MY STRONG personal preference for spring gobbler hunting, my feeling is not shared by every turkey hunter. Many among the fraternity think fall hunting offers the greater challenge. Perhaps they're right. I simply find it much easier to call up a gobbler in the springtime than to toll in any turkey in the fall.

Though turkeys are more abundant in the fall, with spring broods now almost full grown, the birds are more difficult to locate. The fires of their spring passions having cooled, the gobblers have long ceased trumpeting their location to the world, and the mating yelps of the hens have not been heard since early spring. Fall is the time when the hunter must exert his best efforts in searching out the turkeys. He must hunt to the fullest meaning of the word.

Turkeys now travel, feed, and rest in flocks of varying composition. The largest flocks will be comprised of the mother hen and her brood of the year, with perhaps some barren hens and mature hens who have lost their broods. At times several of these family groups will gather into a single large flock. In the fall of 1971 I had reports from reliable sources in New York, Pennsylvania, and West Virginia of flocks that contained upward of fifty birds.

These mixed family flocks constantly vary in composition, coming together, mixing, parting, and rejoining in an ever-shifting pattern. Such temporary flocks may contain a hundred or more birds for short periods of time. When production and survival are high in any year, the young males will leave the family flocks by late November and form flocks of their own. When populations are low, the young males stay with the family group until late December.

The adult gobblers will also have gathered into all-male flocks, with each flock consisting of birds of the same age class. A knowledge of this flocking behavior is of value to the fall turkey hunter in determining his calling procedure on the hunting grounds.

Note the beard dangling from the chest of the turkey gobbler on the right. Although some hens will carry rudimentary beards, this coarse, hairlike growth is the badge of the gobbler. *Photo by Wayne Bailey*

Turkeys feed and travel in flocks, and will cover up to 1,000 acres in following their daily routine. They have a strong flocking instinct, and the most successful technique for fall hunting is the breaking up and scattering of a flock such as this one, followed by calling in individual birds attempting to rejoin the flock. *Photo by Wayne Bailey*

The method most likely to bring success to the hunter in the fall is first for him to find a flock of turkeys, and then to break up and scatter the birds as widely as possible. Turkeys have a strong flocking instinct, and after the flock is scattered the individual members of the flock will—sooner or later—begin calling to each other in an effort to reassemble. In breaking up the flock—by shouting, running toward the birds, shooting into the air, and general hell-raising—the hunter should endeavor to get the birds well scattered in all directions. If the majority of the birds fly or run off in the same direction, they will reassemble at some distance and be difficult or impossible to call in.

With the flock scattered, conceal yourself well and remain in the immediate vicinity of the breakup. The turkeys will invariably attempt to reassemble there. A sure way *not* to get your bird is to go wandering a hundred yards or more away from where the flock broke up, seeking a hiding place that may look better to you. Take advantage of natural cover and stay put.

The turkeys may start calling to each other almost immediately and before you have started calling. Answer this calling as soon as it starts. Listen to the birds at this time. You'll get the finest lessons to be had in turkey calling, and from the best of teachers. In answering their calls, try to make the exact sounds the birds themselves are making.

When a turkey gets close to your hiding place, answer its calling with an occasional *cluck*. You will probably have heard the bird making this sound as it approached. Use this *cluck* only if you are sure that you can make it properly. If you should make the somewhat similar alarm *pert*—a sound all turkey hunters become unhappily familiar with—the show is over!

With the turkey, or turkeys, approaching the assembly point, use as much caution, or even more, than when hunting gobblers in the springtime. Instead of one of the sharpest pairs of eyes in the wilds, honed to razor sharpness and searching you out, there may be three, four, or even more turkeys coming to your call in the fall. Have your gun ready to deliver the shot with the least possible movement. In concealing yourself try to have a clear field of fire in as wide an arc as possible.

Early in the season young turkeys will begin calling and moving toward the assembly point shortly after the flock has been scattered. After a few experiences with hunters, they will display much more caution, and their calling will be at less frequent intervals. Sometimes turkeys will come in to your calling without uttering a sound. Be alert

Note the gleaming and alert eye of the gobbler in the foreground. The wild turkey probably has the keenest vision of all wild things, and can easily make out the form of a man who is absolutely motionless. It behooves the turkey hunter to take every means of concealing himself from those piercing eyes. *Photo by Wayne Bailey*

for these silent and cautious birds. If no answer to your calling is received, or no birds come in to the assembly point after about forty-five minutes to an hour have passed since the flock was scattered, your time will be better spent in seeking another flock.

Failure to locate a flock when hunting turkeys during the fall season does not mean that all possibility of success is ruled out. Scattering the flock and subsequently calling up the birds just happens to be the easiest method of bagging your turkey at this time. Relatively easy, I should say. No turkey hunting is easy, else it would not hold the fascination that it does for those of us who are addicted.

Turkeys are curious birds, and will often answer and come in to your calling to satisfy this great curiosity. Flocks may have been broken up by other hunters, predators, or from some other cause. If it should happen that the flock was scattered in the late afternoon or evening of the previous day, your chances of calling up birds from this flock on the following morning are excellent.

As you travel through the woods searching for a flock, call every three hundred yards or so. Sometimes the birds in an intact flock will answer, and this is an excellent method of locating flocks. It will also often bring a response from a lonesome bird that has been separated from its flock for a considerable time. When hunting by moving from place to place and calling in an attempt to toll up a turkey, use the Kee-Kee run—which is probably the most useful and productive call at this season—and the lost call of the young turkey.

If you have reason to believe that a flock of gobblers is using the area, use the coarse, low-pitched gobbler yelp. This call can be made to perfection with some box calls, and can also be made with the diaphragm and suction calls. The gobblers have no interest at all in the hens and their family flocks at this time of the year, and will answer and come in only to gobbler calls.

When leaves cover the ground, turkeys will make considerable noise when they scratch for food. On a still day this noise can be heard for quite a distance. By listening to it carefully, you can locate the flock and determine its direction of travel. Forget about trying to stalk the flock as a whole! With anywhere from a dozen to fifty pairs of sharp eyes and keen ears constantly on the alert, your chances of taking a bird from an intact flock are slim. Except in extremely open terrain, which is not likely to be found in most turkey country, even the hunter armed with a rifle has little chance of success when dealing with the flock as a unit.

If you can determine the flock's line of travel, try to get ahead on either flank; travel at a considerable distance from the flock, and find a spot where you can conceal yourself. Armed with a shotgun, you'll

Camouflage clothing and a face mask combined with shadows are being used by this hunter to conceal his presence. Gun is the Ithaca Turkey Gun, a combination .222 Remington-12 gauge rifle-shotgun.

have to guess pretty closely as to just where the birds will pass. This is one instance where the rifle, because of its longer range, will out-shine the shotgun. Even if you should miss the shot in this situation, you will have scattered the flock and can then go to work with your call. This ideal situation gives you two chances to score. In their travels turkeys will use certain draws, hollows, coves, and saddles habitually. These favored places can be spotted by the amount of turkey sign such as tracks, droppings, and scratchings found in them. When you stop to rest or eat your lunch, it's a good idea to locate yourself in such a place.

Be particularly alert when passing through an area where you have called earlier in the day. Sometimes a turkey that had heard your earlier calling from a long distance may have come into the area and remained nearby. This, by the way, is also true when calling gobblers in the spring.

This very thing occurred while I was hunting gobblers in New York during the spring season of 1972. As I traveled back through an area where I had called earlier in the morning with no results, I gave out a few hen yelps on my diaphragm mouth call. I was immediately answered by a resounding gobble coming from a short distance to my front.

This was one of those times when I was caught flat-footed by not taking cover before calling. I knew better than to do this, but I really didn't expect an answer, as it was rather late in the morning and I was on my way out of the woods. Using what cover was available, a small stump, I dropped to the ground. The turkey—a beautiful big gobbler—spotted me and departed, uttering what sounded like profanity but was in reality the alarm *pert*. My own language on this occasion has not yet been classified.

I have never called up an entire flock of turkeys, but I have been told by hunters in whom I have every confidence that they have done so on occasion. It's conceivable that a flock that has lost its leader might come in to a good caller. Or perhaps it's just the turkey's innate curiosity that impels the leader to come in and the flock to follow.

Locating a flock of turkeys in their roosting trees in the evening, and subsequently sneaking in on them the following morning to make a kill while the birds are still on the roost, is a practice most good turkey hunters abhor, along with the use of dogs that keep a scattered flock in the trees so that the "hunters" may pot them at their leisure. Both of these practices should be outlawed in every state.

However, the roosting area is a prime location for breaking up a flock preparatory to calling up individual birds. If you are fortunate enough to locate roosting turkeys in the evening, by all means prepare to start your next day's hunt at that point.

Sometimes as you are traveling through the autumn woods in search of turkeys, you will hear turkey yelping that sends you diving for cover and reaching for your turkey call. But try as you will, and putting on the best performance that your ability allows, the turkey will not come in. The bird just stays off at a distance and answers your calling. If this situation remains the same for twenty minutes or more, you would do well to suspect that the "turkey" you are conversing with is a brother hunter.

Under these circumstances it will pay you to be very careful indeed. Careful that you do not injure another hunter—and careful that he does not injure you. Since the turkey, if it is one, has not come in to your calling, there is nothing to lose by advancing rapidly toward the source of the calling, shouting and making plenty of noise as you come. If it should indeed be a turkey, you may get a quick shot as the bird departs. If it should turn out that another hunter is the songster, he will be aware from the commotion that you do not wear feathers.

He may give you a rather peculiar look when you finally heave into view, but a quick explanation of the motives for your unseemly behavior will soon have him smiling and agreeing that you are a very intelligent man indeed. Congratulations on the excellence of his calling will broaden his smiles.

Don't be bashful about disclosing your presence to any other hunter you may see in the woods. Not only is this a much safer procedure for both of you, but it will keep either of you from interfering with the other fellow's hunting plans. Sit down for a moment with the fellow hunter and discuss turkey hunting in general, and your plans for the day. At times you may even learn something from these conversations. I have.

When choosing a spot from which to call, make certain that in addition to providing concealment, it is located so that you can see the approaching turkeys. I lost a chance at a fine gobbler during a recent season because a large fallen tree located about thirty yards in front of the dead treetop in which I was hidden obscured my view. The turkey chose to come as far as the far side of the fallen tree trunk and no further. After stomping around and answering my calls for some ten minutes, he spotted something suspicious and departed, calling down maledictions upon my head.

At times you will hear it advised that merely sitting down in front of a large tree or other object that will break up your outline will provide all the concealment needed in hunting turkeys. This seems to me to be a very foolish and unthinking statement. Consider the fact that you are dealing with a game species possessed of the finest vision to be found in the woodlands. By comparison, deer are blind, requiring some motion on the part of the hunter before they are aware of his presence, even at close range. I've had deer actually walk up to where I was sitting with my back to a large rock and sniff the soles of my boots.

Wild turkeys are equipped with vision that enables them to make out a hunter dressed head to foot in camouflaged clothing and screened by vegetation. This usually occurs after the turkey has been peering in the direction of the hidden hunter for five minutes or so. It has been said that the eye of the turkey can encompass and comprehend in one second what the human eye requires ten seconds to equal. From personal experience I can well believe it.

At times the only cover available in the rather open woods favored by turkeys will be root holes or slight depressions in the forest floor. Turkeys will not approach very dense cover, and the turkey hunter must become adept at using rather sparse means of concealment.

What chance then of the unscreened hunter sitting in front of some object escaping the notice of an approaching turkey? Consider that the hunter must manipulate his call, which entails movements of his hands—unless he is using the diaphragm type—and that he would have to have his gun leveled on the turkey all during its approach. Allah forbid that a mosquito should choose this moment to land on his nose and start drilling operations! The task of the one-armed paperhanger would be child's play by comparison.

It is far better for the hunter to seek out some natural blind such as a downed treetop, boulder, root hole, or log, and if time permits, to further improve his concealment by placing branches, dead tree limbs, brush, or other material where it will do the most good.

When early snows cover the ground in the fall, turkey tracks are, of course, much easier to find, and their age is more easily determined. Fresh tracks look like just what they are. The imprints are sharp, with well-defined edges, and the snow crystals on the small ridges along the edges of the tracks are sharp and unmelted. Older tracks will have rounded edges where they have alternately thawed and frozen, and the snow crystals along their edges will have melted and settled down level with the surrounding snow.

If you should find the tracks of a flock of turkeys in the snow, it is best not to follow directly in their trail. Because of the stark, white background of snow, the birds will be able to see you at extreme range, and they will all run off together so that it is almost impossible to call them in.

Follow the trail from as far to either side as will still allow you to make out the tracks. The turkeys will usually have done some scratching, and these dark spots that are bare of snow will show up well. Here is where a pair of lightweight binoculars are of great value to the hunter. With them you can stay at a considerable distance from the turkey's trail while keeping an eye on its general direction. If possible, stay on ground that is higher than the trail and it will be easier to follow its course.

Keeping the turkey's tracks in sight, slowly advance for a hundred yards or so. Stop and scan the terrain along the trail for any movement. Because of the snow, the birds will be easier to spot as they move along. Take advantage of all cover as you move along parallel to the turkey's route. When the flock is located, the hunting method is similar to that used when a flock has been located by the sounds of their scratching in the leaves.

Get ahead of the flock on its estimated course and prepare an ambush. Again, as in hunting on dry ground, if you should miss the shot or fail to get one, you can still break up the flock and find out just how good you are with the turkey call. Anytime you flush a flock of turkeys from the ground and the birds fly off in the same direction instead of scattering, follow in the direction they have gone. You have a flock located—something that will not happen every day of the season—and you should attempt to follow and scatter them.

Unlike spring hunting, the hunting of turkeys in the fall is an all-day affair. The fall turkey hunter should spend the day from dawn to dark in hunting, learning, and enjoying his time in the woods.

6

Talking Turkey

THE ART OF CALLING the wild turkey is the one aspect of the sport approached by the newcomer with the most misgivings. He looks upon it as a mysterious art, to be mastered only by a select few. This attitude has been fostered by a minority of turkey hunters who wish to give the impression that they are possessed of gifts far greater than those bestowed on the common herd.

Anyone not absolutely tone-deaf can learn to call turkeys! And in short order. He may not be a finished performer—perfection in any art takes time, practice, and experience—but he will be able to use his call well enough to call up turkeys under all ordinary circumstances.

There are only two, or at the most three, absolutely essential calls to be learned. These are the mating yelp of the hen, used in calling up the gobbler in the spring, and the Kee-Kee run and the lost call for fall hunting. All three of these calls are rather easy to master with a good turkey call and a modicum of practice.

The best and easiest way for the beginner to learn to call is by receiving personal instructions from an experienced caller. By sitting with the experienced caller, the beginner will quickly learn the mechanics of calling, and by imitating the tones and cadence produced

INSTRUCTION RECORD NO. 2   33⅓ R.P.M.

famous
wild
turkey
hunters
teach
you

HOW
TO
CALL
WILD
TURKEY

THE
EXPERTS ▶

HARVEY GRAYBILL — 1970 Pa. State Champion
ROGER LATHAM — Mr. Turkey Himself
E. L. WISOR — Expert of the Slate
R. W. BAILEY — One of the Leading
Authorities in the World
DR. LEROY UTT — Sweet Sounding Yelper
THE WILD TURKEY — Best of all with the Yelp,
Cluck, Purr, Gobble, etc.

$2⁴⁹

Penn's Woods Products, Inc., Delmont, Pa. 15626   7008

Though personal instruction from an expert is undoubtedly the best way to learn, turkey calling can be mastered with the help of good calls and recordings by masters of the art.

by the expert, he will be calling well in a remarkably short time. If it is not possible to get personal instructions, there are available from several sources some fine recordings from which calling can be learned. Turkey calling *can* be learned from these recordings.

The only fault to be found with these recordings is that those calls that are absolutely essential to good turkey calling are mixed in with other calls that are nice to know but should not be of concern to the new caller. It's difficult to isolate the essential calls from the fancy doings, but you can do so by replaying those parts of the recording on which the essential calls are given. If there is a tape recorder available, the essential calls can be picked up and isolated on the tape.

In the interest of domestic tranquillity, it would be wise to repair to the basement, den, or other sequestered nook while practicing your calling. Sounds produced while practicing turkey calling are likely to drive other members of the household up the walls! They will not share

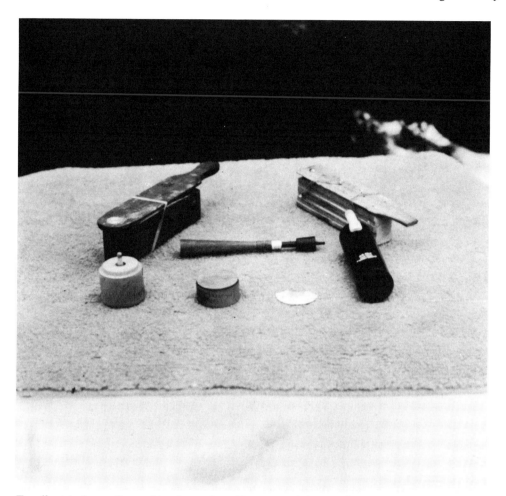

Excellent turkey calls used by the author. *Front row, left to right:* Roger Latham slate call by Penn's Woods; diaphragm call by Penn's Woods; Owl Hooter by P. S. Olt, used to locate roosting turkeys when the hunter has reason not to use the turkey yelp. *Center:* Tom Turpin suction-type yelper by Penn's Woods. This is a modern version of the old turkey wingbone call. *Rear row, left:* the Roger Latham box call by Penn's Woods; right is the M. L. Lynch World Champion box call. This call will produce an excellent imitation of the gobble that will sometimes work when other turkey notes fail to get a response.

your enthusiasm in mastering a new art, and a little forbearance on your part will be the wiser course.

"What type of call should I get?" This is the question most frequently asked by those about to take up turkey hunting for the first time. Let's examine and evaluate the different types of turkey calls that are available.

The old turkey wing-bone call is rarely seen nowadays, but modern versions of this classic type, the suction type "yelpers," are popular with some hunters. A commercial version, the Tom Turpin Yelper made by Penn's Woods Products, is a well-made and compact call. Various homemade calls of this type are sometimes seen, mostly takedown jobs which, when assembled, may be as much as a foot in length. They are made of various combinations of wood, plastic, bamboo, and metal. Some are made with flexible rubber or plastic tubing, which allows them to be coiled up and carried in a pocket.

This is a difficult call for the beginner to learn. It is operated by drawing in the breath while at the same time using the lips in a kissing motion on the mouthpiece. They produce excellent yelps and Kee-Kee runs in the hands of an expert, but I would advise the beginner to become adept with other types of callers before trying the yelper.

The Gibson-type box call, made of various plain and fancy woods, is probably the most popular type of turkey call. This type of call, which more hunters will be found carrying than any other, consists of a hollow wooden box with a pivoting lid secured to one end with a loosely fitted screw or pin. The other end of the lid is formed into a handle so that the lid resembles a small paddle. There is good reason for the popularity of the box call. It is probably the easiest call to use, and it does the job for which it is intended.

The call is operated by stroking one of the thin edges of the box with the underside of the pivoted lid after both have been given a coat of soft chalk. The use of the chalk allows the user to draw clearer tones from the box. The blue carpenter's chalk seems best for this purpose, and it has been said that you can tell a turkey hunter by the smudges of blue chalk on his face, hands, and clothing. By pressing gently on the lid, soft calls are produced; increasing the pressure will produce the loud yelps sometimes desired.

The box call will make every call necessary in turkey hunting except the Kee-Kee run of the young turkey. Some box calls can produce a fairly good imitation of the gobble of the tom turkey. This feature is especially useful for locating gobblers on the roost in the late afternoon and evening. The box produces the loudest of all calls, and is therefore the best call to use for locating distant birds in both spring and fall hunting.

My favorite box is the True Tone made by Penn's Woods Products. It is probably the largest of the box calls and therefore not as easy to carry

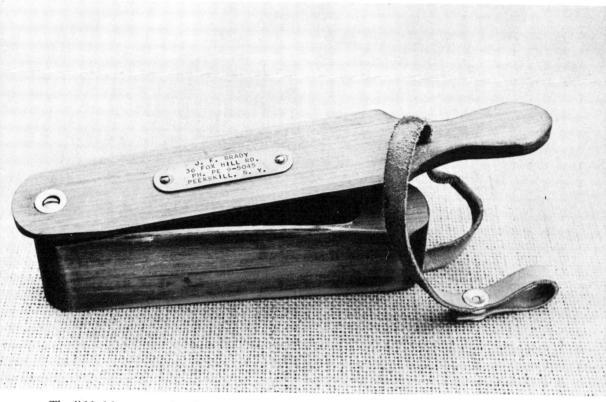

The lidded box type of turkey call is easiest to master, and will make all the calls necessary for turkey hunting with the exception of the Kee-Kee run. The box call will produce the loudest notes, and is especially good for calling to distant turkeys.

in a pocket as some others, but it will send its notes rolling out like a bugle, and is the best call I have used for locating distant birds. I have had gobblers answer my calling from unbelievable distances when using this call in the spring. I've never come across a "squawker" in this model; they are uniformly good. It is not too well adapted for sounding the gobble, but fine yelping can be done with it.

Another favorite is the World Champion box call made by the M. L. Lynch Company. This call produces the finest of gobbles. Of late, it has been necessary to pick over a number of calls in this make in order to find one with the proper tone, but it is one of the finest of calls when you find a good one. This firm produces another fine little call, the Lynch Fool Proof. It is the smallest and most compact of the box calls, easy to use and, as with its larger brother, an excellent call when you locate one with the proper tone.

There are various other makes of box calls on the market, but I have had no experience with them and can therefore make no recommendations. One recommendation I can make is to steer away from the cheap imported boxes sometimes offered as turkey calls. These are abominations.

No turkey hunter should be without a good box call!

The slate-and-peg caller is a great favorite of mine. There are two parts to this call, a small, hollow box, the top of which is covered with a piece of slate, with a bottom of wood having a small hole in its center. The other part consists of a wooden peg about one inch in length, which is set into a hollow knob.

The call is operated by rubbing the peg in a circular motion over the slate-topped box. The slate is kept well sanded with a piece of fine sandpaper. This call will make fine yelps, Kee-Kee runs, and the soft calls necessary to use when the turkey is in close. The tone of the calls can be varied in two ways, by increasing the pressure used on the peg, and by holding the hollow box in the hand under varying degrees of pressure. Next to the diaphragm call, this is the most compact of commercially made calls.

I use the Lynch Jet Slate Call, and it is in my pocket at all times when turkey hunting in both spring and fall. Another fine slate call is the one made by Penn's Woods Products. There are several other makes of slate calls on which I have had good reports, but the above two are the ones I am familiar with. These slate calls are fairly easy to master, and after learning to use the box, I would recommend that the beginner buy a good slate call.

The little diaphragm call will produce the most realistic turkey notes of all. It will make any call but the gobble—although I have heard Jerry Wunz turn out a fair imitation of the gobble with the diaphragm. This call is a small, U-shaped piece of metal, covered by a thin membrane. It is placed inside the mouth, open end foremost, and is held in place against the roof of the mouth by tongue pressure. It is operated by expelling air from the lungs, which causes the membrane to vibrate and produce the desired notes.

One of the greatest virtues of the diaphragm, aside from the natural-sounding notes it produces, is that it requires no movement of the hunter's hands or arms, which might give the show away to the wary and ever-suspicious turkey. Furthermore, this call leaves the hands free to keep the hunter's gun at the ready and pointed in the direction of an approaching turkey.

The slate-type call is a compact and versatile instrument that will produce every note ordinarily needed to call turkeys. Excellent Kee-Kee runs can be sounded with the slate call, and next to the box call, it is the easiest call for the beginner to use.

No call even approaches the diaphragm in its ability to send out the low, sexy notes that will bring a spring gobbler those last few yards and put him under the hunter's gun. Fred Evans, senior wildlife technician with the New York Department of Environmental Conservation, is an artist with the diaphragm call. When describing how a gobbler came in to his calling, Fred told me that "he tried to breed me!"

The diaphragm is a difficult call to master, requiring perhaps more practice than is necessary to become proficient with any of the other calls. I learned to use the diaphragm by keeping one in my pocket during the off-season and popping it into my mouth as I drove along

Some turkey calls used by the author. Left is the Lynch Jet Slate
call. Center is homemade snuffbox call. A commercial version
of the snuffbox call is made by Penn's Woods Products. Right
is the author's favorite, a diaphragm mouth call made by Penn's
Woods Products. This type of call produces the most realistic
notes of all, and being held entirely inside the mouth, there is
no motion of the hands to catch the sharp eye of the turkey.
Another good feature of the diaphragm call is the fact that it
leaves the hunter's hands free to manipulate his gun. In the rear
is the Roger Latham box call by Penn's Woods. This rather large
box will produce the loudest of notes and will call in distant
turkeys.

the highway. This practice has paid off, as I must modestly admit that I'm a pretty fair hand with the diaphragm call.

The only fault of the diaphragm is that the notes produced with it do not carry for any great distance. This is of importance only when trying to toll in a far-out bird. For all other calling it is superb, and learning to use it is well worth the effort.

The diaphragm calls I use are produced by Penn's Woods Products, and are made in two sizes. I use the large "Big Tom" size. Some hunters have told me that this large diaphragm gags them, but the smaller size should take care of this trouble. Both of these calls can be trimmed to fit the individual's needs.

I mention Penn's Woods Products frequently only because their equipment has proven to be first rate in every way. Frank Piper, the president of this firm, is an expert turkey hunter and his love of the game is reflected in the products he produces. There are certainly other fine turkey calls on the market and I use them frequently. For instance, I prefer the Lynch slate call to the similar one put out by Penn's Woods. I believe Frank will forgive me—although he did threaten to throw another make of box call I was carrying into our campfire in North Carolina.

Various other types of calls are sometimes encountered, such as the snuffbox call popular in the Carolinas, the suction diaphragm type made by Leon's—an excellent call, but not as compact as the regular diaphragm, and requiring the use of at least one hand—and assorted calls with separate sound boxes and strikers, none of which are as effective as the slate and peg type.

I would recommend that the beginner obtain a good box call and a slate and peg type. These are the easiest types to operate, and they will reproduce every call necessary. If a turkey hunter were limited to these two types, he would be well equipped. Fine Kee-Kee runs can be made on the slate call, and it will also produce the soft calls to be used when your turkey is almost within range.

All these calls come with instructions for their use. Study closely the instructions having to do with the mechanical operation and care of the call, but try to forget the greater number of the various calls mentioned therein. You will rarely use the vast majority of these calls, and your time would be better spent in mastering the essential calls.

The one essential call necessary for hunting the gobbler in the springtime is the mating yelp of the hen. Fortunately, it is the simplest call of all to imitate, and can be made on any of the various types of calls.

It is a sharp, staccato *keow-keow-keow-keow!* The call is sounded with about one second's interval between the notes. Some calling instructions will state that this call must be made in a series of three, four, six, or some other fixed number of notes.

I have not found that the number of notes in any series is of any importance—as long as there are enough of them. During the past spring season I had occasion to sit and listen to a passionate hen carrying on at a great rate—she had succeeded in stealing away a gobbler on which I was working. Her yelps were sounded in series containing various numbers of notes from five to twelve. Just as soon as she sounded off, my gobbler stopped coming in to my calling, and I remember hoping that when he found the hen she would turn out to be an ugly old bag!

My own method is to sound from eight to ten yelps in a series when prospecting for distant gobblers, and to cut back to about five or six somewhat softer yelps in the series when I have a gobbler interested and coming in to my calling.

I usually start calling fairly softly at first, as there may be a gobbler nearby and the softer notes will sound more natural. This is also true when I have a gobbler located on his roost early in the morning and I have heard him fly down to the ground, or have reason to believe that he has done so.

If there is no response to this soft calling, I will send out several series of eight to ten louder yelps. These yelps will start with an interval of about one second between notes and will end with the notes about one-half second apart. If I manage to raise a gobbler, my calling will still be fairly loud until the approaching turkey has closed the distance between us.

When a gobbler has approached to the point where I can see him, I call very softly, and only enough to keep him interested. At this point I will switch to the diaphragm call so as to obviate any movement of my hands or body, and to allow me to keep my gun in a ready position.

When the gobbler is actually within range, twenty-five to thirty yards, I stop calling altogether. I will resume calling softly by sounding only two or three notes if the turkey shows signs of moving away from me. This is not usually necessary, as the gobbler will have the source of the calling located and will either be in full strut before the supposed hen or peering cautiously about in an attempt to see her.

The instructions received with your call will usually recommend that you sound various soft whines, purrs, or putts when the gobbler is close by. These are very effective if you are capable of making them properly, but I advise that you forego them until you have more experience in calling or have bagged your first gobbler.

If a gobbler answers your first loud calling but fails to come in, or comes in for a certain distance and then hangs up out there or retreats, he can sometimes be taken by making a wide circle around him and calling from a position that is 90 to 180 degrees from your original point. This maneuver is even more effective if the hunter switches calls; box to slate, slate to diaphragm, and so forth.

A trick that sometimes works on a reluctant gobbler is to sound the gobble on a box call that is capable of producing this sound. Convinced that another tom is about to steal the affections of the hen, the up-to-this-point-disinterested gobbler will come storming on the scene in a jealous fury, all caution thrown aside and ready to do battle.

If the fall turkey hunter could make no other call, the Kee-Kee run of the young turkey would be sufficient to put drumsticks on his dinner table. It is the one essential call to learn for success in fall hunting.

Like the young of many species, including man, the voice of the young turkey breaks and changes as the bird approaches maturity. The Kee-Kee will usually start out as a high-pitched yelp and end up on a whistlelike note: *keow-keow-keow-kee-kee-kee-kee-kee-kee!* It may also consist of the *kee-kee* notes alone minus the yelps at the start.

The intervals between notes are shorter than those of the mating hen yelps, being about one-half second between notes. The recordings previously mentioned all give good examples of this call. Listen closely and learn the cadence and sound of the notes.

The Kee-Kee run can be made with the slate and peg, the diaphragm, and the suction-type yelpers. It is the one call that cannot be made with the lidded box call. The beginner's first efforts should be made using the slate and peg, which is the easiest call for him to use in making the Kee-Kee run.

When a flock of turkeys is scattered and the birds start calling to one another, you will hear the young turkeys sounding this Kee-Kee run. Listen to them and answer, using the same notes and rhythm. It is not necessary that you use the exact pitch in which any particular bird is calling. Each turkey will have a slightly different voice, and to the members of the flock your calls will be taken for those of one of the group.

As fall progresses into winter, the Kee-Kee run will be heard less often. The young turkeys mature rapidly, and their calling will now be a fine-pitched yelping in the case of the young hens, with a somewhat lower-pitched yelp coming from the young gobblers who are now about ready to leave the family flock.

Those lost calls of the young turkey will be given with the same rather rapid timing as the Kee-Kee run. Here again, I prefer to use the slate and peg-type caller.

If I could carry but one type of caller for fall hunting, it would be one of these slate and peg types. It will make all the calls necessary for fall hunting, and the yelps and Kee-Kee runs produced are loud enough to be heard by the turkeys at a distance. The box call cannot be used for the Kee-Kee run, and the diaphragm produces notes that are limited in volume.

If the flock you are working on consists of mature gobblers, their yelps will be coarser and lower pitched than those of other turkeys. These older gobblers may not do much yelping in getting together, but may confine their calling to low-pitched clucks. Like all turkeys, however, they will try to reassemble at the place where the flock was broken up.

You may have a longer wait than when dealing with a mixed flock of young turkeys, but the birds will eventually show up. In exceptional cases, especially if the breakup occurred late in the day, mature gobblers may not try to reassemble until the following day. After learning the Kee-Kee run, become familiar in using your call to sound the coarse, low-pitched assembly cluck of the older gobblers.

Read again the chapters on spring and fall hunting. Keep in mind that turkey calling can be learned by almost anyone. Get yourself a good box call and a slate and peg type. In the absence of an experienced caller to help you, obtain some of the good instruction records that are available and practice, practice, practice. Remember that the mastery of any musical instrument takes practice—and a turkey call is essentially a musical instrument despite the unmusical results. When that first turkey comes in to your calling, you will consider your efforts to have been well expended.

Turkey Guns and Loads

UNLIKE THE SOUL-SEARCHING METHODOLOGY with which the upland gunner approaches the acquisition of a shotgun to be used for the taking of grouse, woodcock, quail, and pheasants, choosing a shotgun to be used for turkey hunting is a comparatively simple matter.

Not that just any old gun will do, but the fine points of the drop of the stock at comb and heel, cast off, cast on, length, thickness of comb, curvature—or lack of curvature—of the grip, are of little moment when choosing a turkey gun. For the most part wing shooting is not a skill with which the turkey hunter need be concerned. Almost anytime the turkey hunter must take a shot on the wing, it is an indication that something has gone awry. Either he has goofed or some happenchance of the hunt has caused the turkey to take wing. Wing shots are not the norm in turkey hunting, and the standard American stock dimensions found on over-the-counter shotguns work out very well for this use.

Hunting the wild turkey is rightly compared to big-game hunting rather than to upland gunning, and in some states the turkey is classified as big game; still other states are contemplating the addition of this grand bird to their list of big game. This is a move of which I heartily approve.

Turkeys spend the greater part of their time on the ground, and their comings and goings are mainly accomplished by the use of their legs. Ordinarily, turkeys use their powers of flight only for ascending to and descending from the roost, and to escape some real or imagined danger. Even when danger threatens, they will more often run off on the ground rather than take wing.

Because of the similarity of turkeys to other ground game, the shotgun is used in their hunting in the same manner as the rifle is used for other game of this type; that is, the shotgun is aimed like a rifle rather than being pointed as in wing shooting.

Turkey hunters who use the shotgun in preference to the rifle take great pride in their skill with the turkey call and in the art of concealment. To these hunters, calling their turkey up to within close range—twenty-five to thirty yards—is the essence of the sport.

The shotgun is aimed so as to deliver a dense centered pattern of shot into the area of the turkey's head and neck. When used in this manner, the shotgun is startlingly efficient, usually producing instantaneous one-shot kills. The technique is entirely at variance with wing shooting in the uplands. The turkey hunter marches to the music of a different drummer than do most users of the shotgun.

Shotguns used for turkey hunting range over almost all action types. Pump actions, recoil and gas-operated autoloaders, and both side-by-side and over-under double-barreled guns all find favor with experienced hunters. The cheap single-barrel and bolt-action shotguns, however, are rarely used.

◀

Wild turkeys are primarily ground game, and wing shooting is not a common occurrence when hunting them. On rare occasions a shot at a flying turkey will be presented. Such a shot should not be attempted when the gun is loaded with shot smaller than size 4. Unless smaller shot hits the head or neck, the heavy body feathers will impede the penetration of the shot and the turkey may escape with crippling wounds in the legs and wings. *Photo by Wayne Bailey*

Being blessed with a left master eye, I shoot from the left shoulder, although in all other things I am right-handed. I've been shooting this way since the age of twelve when my dad, a rifleman but no great user of the shotgun, discovered that I was left-eyed and insisted that I change over. From watching the troubles encountered by other "crossed dextrals" in learning to shoot, I've been thankful ever since. Strangely enough, I shoot handguns using my stronger right hand, and well enough to have qualified as expert on both bull's-eye and combat silhouette courses of fire.

Which brings us to this point. I frequently use autoloading and pump-action shotguns that eject fired cases to the right. In all the years that I have been using these guns, I have never been disturbed in the least by the spent shells flying across my face. In fact, I have never been aware of them.

I may be doing them an injustice, but I've always thought that southpaw shooters who complain of this feature of the repeating shotguns have not been keeping their eyes on the target, where they belong. This is of only academic interest today, since we now have available both pumps and autoloaders that eject empty shells to the left, and, of course, we have had for many years the bottom ejection Ithaca Model 37 pump gun.

From my observations the pump gun will more often be found in the hands of turkey hunters than any of the other action types. Of course, this would probably be true of hunters of any other game ordinarily taken with the shotgun. The pump gun is *the* American shotgun.

For the money expended, the pump gun is probably the greatest bargain available. It is at least as reliable and free from troubles as any other action, and will shoot right along with the best of them.

I made a survey of the guns being used by a group of thirteen hunters operating out of one camp during a recent spring turkey season in West Virginia and came up with the following tally. One rifle, one combination rifle-shotgun, one side-by-side double gun, four autoloaders, and six pumps.

Double-barreled shotguns of both the side-by-side and over-under types are used less frequently in turkey hunting than they are on other types of game. The different degrees of choke available in the two barrels are of no advantage when used in this game and, in fact, the double guns have certain disadvantages.

The great Model 12 Winchester pump gun, brought back from retirement by popular demand, is the favorite of many turkey hunters.

The side-by-side doubles carry well in the hand, but the twin tubes do not give the shooter the single alignment that is desirable when the shotgun is aimed like a rifle. The over-under types do not carry well in the hand due to the depth of most actions of this type, and this feature of ease of carrying is important when negotiating the rough terrain found in most turkey country.

A malady afflicting some double guns of both side-by-side and over-under types is poor regulation of the barrels. A perfectly regulated double will theoretically place the pattern fired by one barrel smack dab on top of that fired by its mate at forty yards. Some doubles, even those of high price as well as more modestly priced pieces, will be found to be seriously deficient in this respect. One or both barrels may shoot to the right, left, above, or below the aiming point.

Because the shotgun used on turkeys is aimed like a rifle, poor barrel alignment is a serious fault that should eliminate such a gun from consideration as a turkey gun. Infrequently, a pump or autoloader will be found that does not place its pattern on the mark. Such a gun should be given the same treatment as the poorly aligned double gun. A session with the patterning targets, which will be taken up later, will show up such faults quickly.

The 12-gauge gun is the overwhelming choice of most experienced turkey hunters, and for good reason. A wild turkey gobbler in full spring condition and color is one of the greatest prizes available to the American sportsman. Most confirmed turkey hunters that I know would rather take one of these great birds than the most magnificent elk, moose, or mountain sheep that ever roamed the wilds. Deer are looked upon as minor game, to be hunted when turkeys are not available. These turkey addicts want a gun that can be depended upon to lay that turkey down, and the 12 gauge will usually deliver the goods.

Smaller gauges can be, and are, used by quite a few turkey men. The 16 gauge will frequently be found in the hands of turkey hunters, and of late guns chambered for the 3-inch 20 gauge are being seen. The 2¾-inch 20-gauge guns will be found on rare occasions, usually because it is the only gun owned by a new turkey hunter.

I have never seen a turkey hunter armed with a gun chambering the little 28 gauge and .410 bore shells, and in my opinion, and in the opinion of most experienced turkey hunters, guns smaller than 20 gauge should be barred altogether for use on turkeys. Even the 2¾-inch 20-gauge guns, graceful and easy to carry as they may be, are, because of the limited weight of their shot loads, marginal in a type of shooting that leaves no margin for error.

Because of the small target offered when taking the head-and-neck shot favored by most expert turkey hunters, dense-centered patterns that deliver all the shot possible into this comparatively small area are desirable. Such a shot, taken at forty yards, is a long one. For this reason barrels that will deliver full-choke patterns are found on most turkey guns.

Shotgun barrels do not always deliver patterns consistent with the degree of choke with which they are marked by the manufacturer. With the improved shot shell components now being used, especially the plastic shot containers and wads that keep most of the shot from contacting the bores, many guns will deliver tighter patterns than the nominal choke would indicate. This is all to the good insofar as turkey guns are concerned.

I have a 16-gauge Browning autoloader with a barrel marked *modified* which, with the Magnum 16-gauge load containing 1¼ ounces of No. 6 shot, consistently delivers full-choke patterns of around 72 percent, and I frequently use this gun for turkey hunting. Many older guns will duplicate this tendency toward delivering tighter patterns, those marked *full choke* often giving 85 to 90 percent readings on the patterning board.

The many choke devices on the market that allow the hunter to vary the degree of choke by turning a collet or changing tubes are not as popular as they once were. It has been my experience that unless the utmost care has been taken when installing these devices, they will throw the pattern low—a deadly shotgun sin, for turkeys or any other shooting—or if misaligned, they may put the shot charge over toward Mulligan's Pub. Mulligan doesn't need this, and neither do we.

In any case shotguns for turkey hunting should be patterned in order to determine the character of the pattern and, equally, if not more important, whether or not the gun puts its pattern on the point of aim. The best pattern in the world is useless if it does not hit the target.

I make my patterning targets for turkey guns by drawing silhouettes of a turkey's head and neck on pieces of cardboard. These artistic endeavors will never hang in the Louvre, but their use will give a clear idea about pattern distribution and placement.

The shotgun is the preferred tool of most experienced turkey hunters. Shown here is author's 16-gauge Browning autoloader. Although barrel is marked "modified," this gun delivers full-choke patterns with the 1¼-ounce 16-gauge Magnum loads.

▶

It pays to determine character of the patterns delivered by a shotgun and whether or not these patterns center on the point of aim. Patterning targets such as this one used by the author, while admittedly no work of art, will quickly show up any deficiencies.

There is some difference of opinion among turkey hunters regarding proper shot sizes to be used in taking turkeys. A minority of hunters prefer No. 2 shot on the theory that the turkey is a hard bird to kill, being tenacious of life to an astonishing degree, and that the energy and penetration inherent in the large shot is needed to do the job. These large-shot exponents usually shoot at the turkey's body.

Most turkey hunters now favor the head-and-neck shot, and prefer no shot larger than No. 4s. The dense swarm of small shot striking the head and neck acts like a bolt of lightning, usually anchoring the turkey on the spot. Combined with a pattern that is tighter than tight, they produce what every sportsman worthy of the name desires, a clean kill or a clean miss.

Most turkey hunters that I know and hunt with use heavy loads of No. 6 or 7½ shot. I usually carry a stiff load of 7½s in the chamber of my gun for the first shot, with follow-up loads of 4s in the magazine for use in the unlikely event that the first load is not effective.

The larger No. 4s will give the good penetration and energy needed to bring down the bird if by some mischance it should run off or take wing after the first shot aimed for the head and neck. No. 2 shot delivers patterns that are too loose for this work.

A large variety of loads are suitable for turkey hunting when fired from a well-aimed barrel. The 3-inch Magnum 12-gauge loads containing 1⅝ and 1⅞ ounces of shot are more than adequate. Guns chambered for the 3-inch Magnum 12-gauge loads average being heavier in weight than those chambered for 2¾-inch shells. Since much turkey hunting involves a lot of travel afoot over some pretty rough country, gun weight can be a pretty important factor in hunter comfort.

A fairly light gun is recommended even when stiff loads are used. Since only a few shots will be fired, the recoil factor is not important. A 12-gauge gun chambered for the 2¾-inch shell is probably the best all-around choice.

If the hunter feels that he must have a Magnum load, he would be advised to try the 2¾-inch Magnum 12 loaded with 1½ ounces of shot. However, the standard 12-gauge high velocity load containing 1¼ ounces of shot was the heaviest load available for many years, and thousands of turkeys have been taken with it. It is my standard for turkey hunting under all conditions.

There seems to be some confusion even among knowledgeable gunners as to the terms "high base" shells and "high brass" shells. The high base is found inside standard velocity target and field loads, and is not

Autoloading shotguns are popular for turkey hunting, especially by those who prefer the heavy-recoil magnum loads. The gas-operated actions like this Garcia-Beretta AL-2 absorb much of the recoil.

visible when handling the loaded shell. High brass is found on high velocity and Magnum shells just forward of the head, and is merely an identification mark.

These more powerful high velocity and Magnum shells have a *low base* inside in order to make room for their heavier shot charges. Strangely enough, the lower velocity target and field loads generate higher breech pressures than the high velocity and Magnum loads. The milder recoil of the target and field loads is due to the lighter shot charges with which they are loaded.

In 16-gauge guns to be used for turkey shooting, the Magnum load containing 1¼ ounces of shot should be used. This same 1¼-ounces load is available in the 3-inch Magnum 20 gauge. So, we have the 12, 16, and the 3-inch 20-gauge all loaded with the entirely adequate 1¼-ounces shot load. It would seem then that there is no choice between them. However, for some reason, the manufacturers seem bound to put out 3-inch Magnum 20-gauge guns that average heavier in weight than the 16-gauge guns, and edge right up to the 12-gauge guns in the weight department.

The factory boys seem to have seen the error of their ways of late, and we now have guns chambering the 3-inch 20-gauge round that are light in weight and graceful. Remington now has a lightweight, mahogany-stocked Model 870 pump gun chambering this shell, and Ithaca has some imported autoloaders for the 3-inch 20, which should make fine turkey guns.

All in all, I prefer the 12 gauge. Shells are available in every crossroads store in the land, and some fine guns are available in this gauge that are light and comfortable to carry. It will be a long time—if ever—before the 12 gauge is replaced in the affections of the American gunner.

Turkey hunters should choose a gun with the shortest barrel that will deliver the required tight, dense patterns. Because of the somewhat cramped positions and tight quarters assumed by the hunter in concealing himself from a bird that is only twenty-five to thirty yards away, a short, compact gun will be appreciated. In most makes of repeaters, this will be a 28-inch full-choke or a 28- or 26-inch modified barrel if the latter will produce full-choke patterns. I own an Ithaca Model 37 pump gun in 12 gauge, which has a 26-inch full-choke barrel. This is the shortest factory full-choke barrel that I know of, and this gun with its 6¾-pound weight makes an ideal turkey gun.

Shotguns chambering the 3-inch 20-gauge magnum shell, such as the Remington Model 870 pump gun, are excellent for use on turkeys.

Guns chambered for the 2¾-inch 20-gauge shells should be stoked with nothing less than the Magnum load in this length, which contains 1⅛ ounces of shot. Preferably, No. 7½ shot should be chosen in order to assure a decent pattern density at the target. Even so, this load is marginal for use on turkeys, and if the gunner desires a 20-gauge gun he should by all means go to the 3-inch round in this gauge.

Adding it all up, the ideal shotgun for turkey hunting is a short, compact, lightweight gun, chambering a shell containing a minimum of 1¼ ounces of shot, and preferably having the riflelike single alignment found on the pump gun, autoloader, and over-under double barrel. By lightweight, I mean a maximum of 7 pounds. The barrel should be capable of producing dense-centered, full-choke patterns. Guns meeting these criteria are available in 12, 16, and 3-inch 20-gauge chamberings.

Because of the recoil generated by the heavy loads used, and the fairly light weight of the ideal turkey gun, a good sponge-rubber recoil pad will be appreciated. Shots at turkeys are delivered in a deliberate manner, akin to those made with a rifle.

At times the turkey hunter will shoot from the prone position. He will rarely be standing in the rather loose-jointed position of the wing shooter, which helps in great measure to absorb recoil. The recoil pad on a turkey gun is not merely decorative, it is an entirely functional accessory.

My shotguns used for turkey hunting are fitted with carrying slings of the detachable type. This accessory performs two functions. Carrying the gun in the hand over rough and oftentimes mountainous terrain can become tiresome, and it is a relief to be able to sling the gun from a shoulder. At times both hands will be needed when ascending or descending steep slopes, and slinging the gun out of the way is the only way to have both hands free.

When a turkey has been located, and I have concealed myself in some hidey-hole preparatory to calling, the sling is removed and placed in a pocket of my jacket so that it does not catch on branches or brush and impede gun movement. The usefulness of the sling does not end here.

When a turkey has been taken, the hunter faces the problem of getting it out of the woods. Often he will be many miles from his camp or car, and carrying a 20-pound bird in the hand can become burdensome.

Carrying a turkey for any great distance in the hand can become
extremely tiresome. Here is where a detachable gun sling serves
a double purpose by being used as a carrying device.

In addition to its primary function of allowing the hunter to carry his gun comfortably, the carrying sling will do double duty as a means of toting out a downed turkey.

Two leather thongs can be fastened to each end of the sling, and then tied securely to the turkey's legs and neck. The turkey can then be slung from the shoulder and carried in comparative comfort. It is also a good idea to carry some lengths of string for use in binding the bird's wings close to its body so that they do not flop about and catch on protruding brush.

Personally, I like ribs on the barrels of my turkey guns. They add but little weight, and seem to give a better sighting plane for the riflelike use of the gun. I also like a middle sight on the rib, which seems to be an aid in sighting. The middle sight is easily installed if the gun does not come so equipped. However, most hunters get along very well without the aid of a rib, and it is strictly a matter of personal preference.

Ideally, a turkey gun should throw its pattern rather high in relation to where the front sight is held, so that a clear view of the turkey's head is seen by the hunter. For this reason a few hunters use trap guns, which are stocked so as to place their patterns high. These are long-barreled and rather heavy pieces that are not too comfortable to carry. When the hunter arrives at the point where the niceties of fitting out a gun for turkeys is of importance, he can have a straight stock—less drop at comb and heel—fitted to his gun so as to give this high pattern placement.

The combination rifle-shotguns of the over-under and double-barreled drilling types are favored by some avid turkey hunters. These guns give the hunter the opportunity to take the occasional long shot by using the rifled barrel. They are more useful for fall hunting than for the hunting of spring gobblers, although even here, a rare long shot will be presented.

I took my spring gobbler this year with the Ithaca Turkey Gun, an over-under type with a 12-gauge shot barrel over a rifled barrel chambered for the .222 Remington cartridge. I used the shot barrel to collect my bird at about twenty-five yards. Savage also makes a medium-priced gun of this type, their Model 24-V, combining a rifled barrel for the .222 Remington cartridge and a shot barrel chambering the 3-inch 20-gauge load.

The drilling-type guns, with usually two side-by-side shot barrels with a rifled barrel underneath them, are rather expensive items, usually selling from around six hundred to a thousand dollars or more. These guns are not too rich for my appetite, but they are entirely too rich for my pocketbook.

The turkey hunter who prefers to use a rifle has a wider choice of guns and loads than the shotgun man. None of the .22 rimfire cartridges,

Author's Ithaca Turkey Gun. Designed specifically for hunting turkeys, the top barrel is chambered for the 2¾-inch 12-gauge shotshell. Bottom rifled barrel is chambered for the .222 Remington cartridge.

◄

Another combination rifle-shotgun used by many turkey hunters is the Savage Model 24-V chambered for the 3-inch 20-gauge magnum shotshell and the .222 Remington rifle cartridge.

including the rimfire Magnums, are powerful enough to kill a turkey with certainty. They will frequently only wound a bird, which then goes off and dies. Their use should be barred in every state. The 5mm Remington Rimfire Magnum may be suitable, and from its published ballistics I believe it may be, but I have not used this cartridge personally, nor have I heard any reports of its use on turkeys.

Many center-fire cartridges can be used successfully, and in any type of action. This statement must be qualified by the further statement that most cartridges, in order to be suitable for turkey hunting, must be handloaded *down* from their factory ballistics, that is, they must be loaded so as to give much less delivered energy at the target.

It is not my intention here to go into a list of loads for various cartridges. Any rifle shooter who has advanced to the stage where he is reloading his cartridges can pick a load from the various manuals available. Since his goal will be to assemble a load that is on the low side as far as velocity and pressure are concerned, he is not likely to run into any trouble from overloads. His main concern should be to develop an accurate load without overkill, and this overkill is the feature that rules out most factory cartridges for turkey hunting.

The one exception to the general rule as far as factory-loaded cartridges are concerned is the .22 Hornet cartridge. In his later years this was the favorite cartridge of Henry E. Davis, author of *The American Wild Turkey*. During a hunting career that spanned almost three quarters of a century, Davis, with the possible exception of Fleetwood Lanneau, probably took more turkeys than any other hunter in comparatively modern times.

Davis, while extolling the superiority of the shotgun for most turkey hunting, preferred to use the rifle. The .22 Hornet cartridge seems made to order for turkey hunting. The .222 Remington cartridge, which I carried in the rifle barrel of the shotgun-rifle combination Ithaca Turkey Gun this past spring, was handloaded to give almost the exact ballistics of the .22 Hornet cartridge.

Turkey rifles should be fitted with scope sights. Many shots at turkeys will be under the less-than-ideal lighting conditions of early morning and late afternoon, and the scope will allow clear aim at targets that would be impossible with iron sights. Since the range at which turkeys are usually taken with a rifle rarely exceeds one hundred yards, a four-power glass with good light-gathering powers and resolution is ideal.

The best aiming points when using a rifle are at the wing butt on side shots and at the juncture of the turkey's neck and body on frontal shots.

A fine turkey rifle, the Sako Vixen is chambered for the .222 Remington round.

The rifle is the preferred tool of some experts for all turkey hunting. These are usually expert rifle shots who enjoy precision shooting. Under certain conditions of terrain, it is the logical choice for all. Author's turkey rifle, above, is chambered for the .222 Remington cartridge and is equipped with a six-power telescope sight. For use on turkeys, the .222 cartridge is loaded down to give the ballistics of the .22 Hornet cartridge.

On shots that must be taken at turkeys facing away from the shooter—not recommended if they can be at all avoided—the best aiming point is at the middle of the back.

Don't try for a head shot. It's very difficult to connect with this small target, which is usually in motion. The usual result is a spooked turkey and a lost opportunity. Wait until the turkey moves and presents a better target.

Since the opportunities to take turkeys with the rifle will most often be had under rather dim lighting conditions, the telescope sight should have a reticule of a type that can be easily seen against the target. Plain cross hairs in the fine-to-medium thicknesses will many times be lost to view in a confusing welter of branches and brush.

Coarse cross hairs are good, but even better are the various types of reticules that have rather heavy cross hairs at the edge of the field of view, which either taper to medium thickness in the center or abruptly change from very heavy to medium thickness.

A fine reticule for use on a turkey rifle is the Command Post supplied on Bushnell scopes. By turning a knurled ring, the hunter has at his command either a medium cross hair for use in good light, or a tapered post reticule that will show up under the most difficult light conditions.

Everything considered, the hunter who is just starting his career as a turkey hunter should choose the shotgun for his first forays afield. He will be properly equipped for 90 percent of the hunting conditions he will encounter.

After a few years of experience, he may then decide that because of some local conditions of terrain or game behavior on certain of his hunting grounds, a rifle would be the more efficient tool.

The lightweight Ithaca Model 37 pump gun is popular with many turkey hunters.

Two shotguns much used by the author for turkey hunting. On the left is a 16-gauge Browning autoloader. Right is an Ithaca Model 37 pump gun with 26-inch full-choke barrel. Both guns have ventilated ribs that seem to be aids to accurate gun pointing.

8

Clothing and Related Items

AT TIMES the sight of a turkey hunter coming forth from the woods is an experience calculated to set babies to wailing and otherwise tractable horses to running wild.

Behold The Turkey Hunter! Clad in camouflaged clothing from head to foot, his face like as not smeared with green and brown paste or striped and smudged with charcoal, his face mask entwined about his cap like a turban, he is indeed a fearful sight to look upon.

The true turkey hunter accepts the sometimes vacuous stares of less fortunate folks with serene equanimity. If he should meet an upland gunner seeking grouse and woodcock, and this poor fellow skirts his path in a wide and cautious arc, eyes rolling, and gun gripped with knuckles white, he will salute him with a cheerful wave of his hand so as to assure him that this is no woodland demon sprung forth from the earth, but merely a hunter of another breed, pursuing his strange and devious ways.

It must be admitted that the turkey hunter is not an exponent of sartorial spendor. His choice of garments is dictated by the practical requirements of his sport. No wearer of the Tyrolean hat, leather-faced britches, and Norfolk shooting jacket is he.

Starting from the ground up, the first and most important item of the turkey hunter's apparel to consider is footwear. Nothing will add so much to hunter comfort as a well-fitted and well-broken-in pair of shoes or boots. Nothing will cause so much misery as ill-fitted and uncomfortable footwear.

The turkey hunter may travel for many miles over rough and broken country in his daily forays. Especially in fall hunting, he will be on his feet from daylight until dark. Feet will swell after a few hours and miles in the field, and footwear larger in size than that normally worn for everyday wear should be selected.

How much larger? The answer to this will have to be determined by the individual. One thing I can say is that you cannot depend on the nominal shoe size marked on the footwear. It would be simple to state that if the individual wears, let us say, a size 9 dress shoe, he should choose a hunting boot or shoe in size 9½ or 10. Since heavier socks than normal will and should be worn, they will take up quite a bit of room. Added to this is the fact that the footwear will stretch slightly with use.

My own system when having shoes fitted is to wear a very heavy pair of wool socks over the somewhat lighter ones I will ordinarily wear while hunting. This allows for the normal swelling of the feet from exertion. Shoes are then selected of a size that will give a snug fit all around.

There is a tendency to select shoes that feel "good" in the store. This will usually result in buying shoes that will actually be too large after they have stretched, and stretch they will. Footwear that is too large will allow the feet to slide back and forth, particularly when traveling up and down hill, and the shoe or boot to move up and down at the heel.

These two conditions will result in sore toes and heels, and a chafing of the balls of the feet. Select footwear that feels a mite on the tight side when worn over the combination of medium- and heavy-weight socks in the shop. Remember, you will not be wearing the heavier socks while hunting.

Ordinarily, extremes of weather will not be encountered in spring or fall turkey hunting, and leather footwear that is on the light side should be chosen. The leather should be no higher than necessary to protect the ankles from stones and brush. Even the 8- or 9-inch bird-shooter boots are unnecessary.

A light, comfortable pair of 6-inch-high leather shoes will be suitable for all but rainy or snowy weather. The turkey hunter will be more concerned with keeping his feet cool than in keeping them warm, and he will have little need for insulated footwear. Lug soles of the Vibram type are practical for travel over most of the terrain encountered in turkey hunting, and the wedge-shaped crepe soles are also good.

I have for years been wearing the light, 6-inch Dunham Tyrolean shoes, not only for turkey hunting but for dry-weather deer hunting and upland gunning as well. These fine shoes are made of soft leather, are fully lined with glove leather, and have a bellows tongue that keeps out twigs, gravel, and other debris. They may be obtained with either Vibram lug soles, or the crepe-wedge type. I recommend them highly.

If you spend six days in turkey hunting, it will rain on at least two of them. Guaranteed! Spring and fall are both rather rainy seasons, and the turkey hunter should be prepared to cope with this in the footwear department. Here again lightweight equipment is needed. I go for a boot that comes up higher on the leg than my leather footwear. Rain makes puddles and raises the height of small watercourses, and I like to barge right on through them.

A 10- to 12-inch all-rubber pac of the noninsulated type will keep the feet dry and will not be so heavy as to become tiresome when worn all day. My personal choice here is the all-rubber pacs bearing the Ball-Band trademark. This is an extremely lightweight pac of high quality.

Medium-weight woolen socks will cushion the feet and absorb perspiration. Lightweight socks do not provide enough cushioning effect, and tend to wrinkle and chafe the feet. Heavy socks, though fine for cushioning the feet, are just a little too warm for the temperatures usually prevailing during turkey seasons.

I usually carry an extra pair of socks during fall hunting. Most of the day will be spent in the woods, and I like to change socks after lunch. If there is a brook or pond nearby, I'll wash my feet and dry them thoroughly with paper towels or napkins. This little noonday rite pays surprising dividends in comfort.

Extra attention should be given to your toenails before venturing into the woods. Nails that are too long will be the source of acute discomfort when your foot slides forward in the shoes or boots while descending slopes; and they will quickly wear holes in the socks, thus compounding the felony.

If I seem to have given an inordinate amount of space to this subject of footwear and care of the feet, remember that the feet are the platform from which the turkey hunter will launch much of his activities. Their importance cannot be stressed too highly.

Unlike the upland gunner who is constantly battling briars, thornbushes, and assorted obstacles to his progress, the turkey hunter for the most part encounters fairly open terrain. He generally has no need for the leather- or canvas-faced trousers so necessary to the upland gunner. He can therefore be well suited with a lightweight pair of comfortable trousers with good, deep pockets. Light cotton work pants of a brown, gray, or greenish color are fine. Some hunters wear trousers in a camouflage pattern that matches their jacket.

There is nothing wrong with these camouflage britches, but I have a theory—unproven—that the solid color trousers, combined with a camouflage jacket and headgear, offers even better concealment to the hunter. With this combination his upper half seems disembodied from the lower when viewed from a distance. There is no distinct human outline. The legs, encased in dull brown, gray, or green, seem to blend in with the stumps, rocks, and logs on the forest floor, while the upper body and head blend in with the upstanding brush and leaves.

The turkey hunter's jacket or coat should, of course, be in a camouflage pattern and be made of lightweight cloth. I favor the patterns of brownish hues rather than the greens. In both spring and fall the major background colors are those provided by fallen leaves, and the brownish patterns seem to blend better with them. In practice I hedge all bets and wear a jacket that is reversible and allows a choice of predominantly brown or green hues, even though I almost invariably wear it brown side out.

Headgear can be any camouflaged cap or hat. Here again, in the interest of breaking up the human outline, I like my headpiece to be of a different pattern than that of the jacket. All this may seem like splitting hairs, but considering our gimlet-eyed adversary, I operate on the theory that every little bit helps.

Face masks and gloves made of camouflaged netting are of distinct aid in hiding the hunter. You have probably noticed at times that the first discernible aspect of another hunter is his face and hands. Some hunters do not like the face masks, claiming that the netting distorts their vision when shooting. Many of these hunters will cover their faces with one of the camouflage pastes on the market, which come in shades of brown and green, or will streak their face with charcoal or burnt cork.

In the more northerly turkey ranges, the air can be quite chilly at the early hours when hunters are first on the prowl. I usually wear a down-filled undershirt beneath my jacket, removing it as the air warms or as I become warmer when climbing a steep-sided ridge. It is then

Screened from the sharp eyes of the wild turkey by his camouflaged clothing, this successful hunter bagged his bird at a range
of twenty yards.

stuffed into my small hunting pack, to be retrieved and donned again if the weather should turn colder. One of these down-filled shirts, vests, or a light woolen jac-shirt should be part of every turkey hunter's wardrobe.

Two-piece long johns are a comfort in chilly weather, and of late I wear the bottom portion of this great invention most of the time when I am out after turkeys. If it is really cool, I'll also wear the uppers. I like the Duofold brand made of two light layers of cloth, which provides an insulating air space.

Rain will fall! If there is anything more miserable looking in the woods than a rain-soaked turkey, it is an equally rain-soaked turkey hunter. I don't ordinarily carry rain gear while hunting (on the off chance that it might rain), but when weather reports suggest the possibility of rain, into my pack goes a rainproof parka. Mine is a reversible model, olive drab on one side, camouflage pattern on the other.

If it is actually raining when I start out, I'll more likely be clad in a complete foul-weather suit with separate pants and a hooded jacket. This suit is also reversible, olive drab-camouflage pattern. With all-rubber pacs on my feet, this outfit keeps me at least comfortably dry all day.

Like most completely waterproof clothing, body moisture will condense on the inner surfaces after a few hours, and some hunters prefer to let the rain do its worst and wear only waterproof footwear and perhaps a rain hat. Their theory is that since they are going to get wet either way, they prefer to let the rain do it.

If the turkey hunter knows he will be hunting at high altitudes during an early spring or late fall season, it might be wise to take insulated footwear along in order to be prepared for all eventualities. During an early April trip into the mountains of West Virginia a few years ago, we awoke one morning to find four inches of snow on the ground, and the air temperature at 28 degrees. I was glad that I had tucked a pair of rubber-bottomed, leather-topped pacs with thick felt liners behind the spare tire in my trunk.

It is a most comfortable feeling to be able to change into some "relaxin'" clothes on returning to camp, cabin, or lodge after a hard day's hunt. A pair of light slacks, a lightweight jacket, and a pair of sport shoes or moccasins are well worth the little room they take up when packing for a hunting trip. A couple of light sport shirts will complete the outfit.

9
Incidental Equipment

THERE ARE CERTAIN ITEMS of equipment which, while only incidental to the turkey hunter's main effort, will do much to bring his hunt to a successful, comfortable, and safe conclusion. These small items sometimes make all the difference between an enjoyable day in the woods and absolute misery.

We are born with only one pair of eyes, and, unfortunately, they are irreplaceable. The outdoors abounds in hazards to the eyes, and it is a smart idea indeed to provide all available protection possible to these important organs. A good pair of shooting glasses will protect the hunter's eyes from the branches that often snap back with considerable force while traveling through the woods, and from the sharp stubs of broken brush often encountered.

I started wearing shooting glasses after a friend suffered an injury when he turned suddenly at the flush of a grouse, and a sharp branch tip lacerated his eye badly enough to require medical attention. Needless to say, that was the end of that day's grouse hunting.

The best type of shooting glasses are those with lenses large enough to cover the entire area around the eyes. The lenses should be of impact-resistant glass or strong plastic. Plastic lenses scratch rather easily, and these scratches then interfere with clear vision. However, plastic glasses are comparatively inexpensive and can be replaced when they become scratched so badly as to be unusable. Low-priced eye protection is far better than no protection at all.

For the hunter who requires optical correction, shooting glasses are available ground to prescription. Lenses of green, neutral gray, and yellow can be obtained, and I usually carry two pairs, one with green lenses and the other with yellow. The yellow lenses filter out the blue component in daylight, and give an apparent increase in contrast on dull days and in early morning and late evening. The green lenses are worn under bright daylight conditions.

The turkey hunter in particular depends in great measure on his sense of hearing. Though I cannot, of course, recommend the wearing of earplugs or muffs, a little attention to the protection of your ears is well advised. When choosing a calling position, examine the surrounding brush and branches for any sharp stubs that might enter the ear and cause injury. Likewise, if you should cut or arrange any brush around your hiding place, be certain that none of it is placed so as to endanger your ears or eyes. Though earmuffs or plugs are out of place while actually hunting, their use is highly recommended when practicing shooting or when patterning your shotgun or sighting in your rifle.

Studies have shown that the repeated exposure of the unprotected ear to the sounds of gunfire will cause an irreversible loss of hearing. There are on the market many devices for the protection of the ears from loud and repeated noise. The best of these are the muff types with a band that fits over or behind the head to hold them in place. Anyone who does much shooting should wear some sort of ear protection.

As mentioned in Chapter 5, Fall Turkey Hunting, I carry a pair of lightweight binoculars. These will save the hunter many steps when he wishes to examine objects at a distance, and I've used binoculars to pick out turkeys while traveling through the woods in the fall. I've found the Bushnell Custom Compact binoculars of six power to be excellent for all woods hunting. These glasses weigh only 11 ounces, have good resolution, and provide a brilliant image. They are indeed compact, as their name implies, being a mere 3⅛ inches high and 4¼ inches wide.

The turkey hunter should carry a knife, but there is no need for the large sheath knives carried by big-game hunters. The smallest sheath knives are suitable, but a folding pocket knife with two blades of the type known as a trapper's knife will do all the cutting jobs necessary, including the field dressing of turkeys.

Keep the knife sharp. A dull knife is a dangerous instrument that will at times slip instead of cutting into whatever is being worked upon. The off-course blade of a dull knife seems to have an affinity for cutting into the precious hide of the user.

I despise bulging pockets when traveling through the woods. To me they impart a most uncomfortable feeling and lend to the hunter the appearance of being a potato smuggler. For these reasons I first started carrying a light hunting pack.

Feeling especially encumbered one fall day by the bulging contents of the pockets of both my trousers and jacket, I decided to take an inventory. Here is what I found.

Two sandwiches, an orange, a box call, a slate and peg call, two diaphragm calls, a match safe, a compass, pocket knife, two lengths of

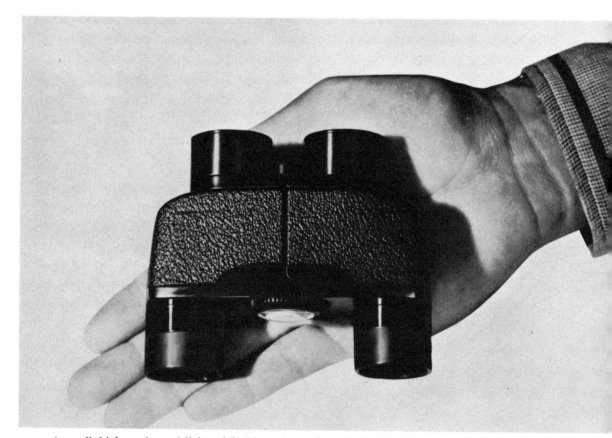

A small, high-grade, and lightweight binocular such as the Bushnell Custom Compact is a fine and useful addition to the turkey hunter's gear.

rawhide thong, 35mm camera with lens shade, a square of plastic sheeting, five shotshells, toilet paper, a plastic bottle of insect repellent, flashlight, a folded topographic map, four Band-Aids, handkerchief, a pair of camouflage gloves, camouflage face mask, two fire-starter cubes, folding drinking cup, tobacco pouch, corncob pipe, eight dollars and twenty-two cents, a card case containing licenses, and car keys.

I determined right then and there to find another and better way to carry those items that need not be immediately available. After diligent searching in various shops, I found a small, dark green nylon pack called a "Daypack." This little pack is waterproofed with an interior urethane coating, weighs three quarters of a pound, and measures 16 by 12 by 5 inches. It has a drawstring top closure and an outside pocket with a covered zipper closure.

This small pack has proven to be indispensable, and I have since acquired another in blaze-orange color for deer hunting. Into it go all those items that will only be required at infrequent intervals, such as lunch, extra shells, camera, extra calls, and the like. When the day grows warmer, into the pack goes whatever clothing I have removed, and when reports of impending rainy weather have been received, I place my rainproof parka in the pack. Extra socks and items likely to be used frequently—camera, drinking cup, toilet paper—are carried in the outside pocket.

For obvious reasons a hunter should never enter the woods without matches for starting a fire. These should be carried in a screw-top match safe and be used only for emergencies. If you smoke, carry a separate match supply for this purpose. I carry several of the commercial fire starters in my pack. These make the building of a fire much easier, even with damp wood.

Your flashlight will be used when entering the woods before daylight, mostly during spring gobbler seasons. A good substantial two-cell type is all that is needed; it takes up little room in the pack when the need for its light has passed.

At times, despite all precautions, snow, mud, or other debris will lodge in the gun barrel. Firing the gun with an obstruction in the barrel is an invitation to disaster. The least that can happen is a ruined barrel, and the result may well be a ruined hunter. Unless the obstruction can be removed, your hunting is over for the day or until the barrel is cleared.

A light pack will carry all the items the hunter usually stuffs in
various pockets in a much more comfortable manner.

Most obstructions can be removed from a shotgun barrel with an improvised cleaning rod cut from a small, straight sapling or branch. I carry a few cleaning patches in my pack to remove whatever remains after the main obstruction has been cleared.

Clearing an obstruction from a rifle barrel with such an improvised rig is an almost impossible job. When hunting with a rifle, I carry a jointed aluminum cleaning rod that weighs next to nothing in the pack, together with a few patches of the proper size. You may never need this equipment, but when and if you do, you'll need it badly.

I usually carry about six extra rounds of ammunition with me while hunting. These are in addition to the rounds carried in the gun. This is sufficient for all but the most extraordinary circumstances. If I am hunting in a real wilderness area, I may slip six more rounds into the pack.

My first-aid equipment consists of some Band-Aids, a few breakable ampules of tincture of Merthiolate, and a roll of one-inch adhesive tape. The tape is useful should a shoe or boot start to chafe the foot. It should be applied *before* a blister appears. The tape has other uses too, such as a temporary repair to a rip in rain gear, jacket, or trousers. Any sizable rip in the trousers should be repaired immediately. Torn trousers can be dangerous. I found this out the hard way when I was sent sprawling full length by a foot-high stub that caught in just such a rip. Fortunately, I was not injured, but there is a slight dent in one of my gun stocks to remind me to be wary of ripped trousers.

Wooden box calls can be fragile things, a fact of life brought home to a friend when his foot came down on his favorite Lynch box as he rushed toward his downed turkey. I usually carry an extra box call in my pack, not only as a spare, but because I sometimes like to change calls and for some reason may not wish to go to the slate or diaphragm.

Bugs bite. This bit of knowledge comes to all who spend any appreciable time in the outdoors rather early in their careers. Especially in the spring, the turkey hunter will make frequent contact with mosquitoes, gnats, black flies, midges, punkies, no-see-ums, and, in fact, the whole gamut of biting insects. There have been times when I regarded my supply of insect repellent as being more important than my gun.

Some of the camouflage pastes used for hiding the face and hands contain an insect repellent as one of their ingredients. Ticks, like some politicians, can be particularly pervasive pests. When hunting in territory where they are abundant, it helps somewhat to keep the trousers tight to the shoes or boots with rubber bands. Cuffs of shirts and jackets should also be kept closed and tight, and the neckbands of shirts and jackets likewise.

Despite all your efforts, some ticks will get through and embed themselves in your hide. A thorough inspection of your body is the only sure method of eliminating all these nasty little visitors. On a recent hunt in the lowland area of North Carolina, our group held a tick pickin' party each evening, during which the members inspected each other for the presence of the little brothers. As one fellow said, "This is no time to be bashful." Fortunately, most turkey hunting areas are practically tick free, and these precautions are necessary only in heavily infested regions.

I've been experimenting lately with some of the adhesive camouflage tapes intended for application to hunting bows by applying it to my shotgun barrels. The tape comes in just about the right length and width, and does a good job of making the barrels inconspicuous and cutting reflections. I have also tried the camouflage pastes intended for application to the skin, and these too adhere well to the barrel and are easily removed with soap and water.

Because I am an outdoor writer, a camera is one of the tools of my trade. Photographs, therefore, are not just things that are nice to have, but are absolutely indispensable. A camera goes with me whenever I am hunting, fishing, or just roaming around in the outdoors. Incidents happen in a flash which, if not recorded by the camera then and there, are lost forever.

Though not vital to the sportsman, pictures of the hunt, the game, the country, companions in the field, the camp or lodge will be treasured mementos for years to come. In these days of simplified and automatic exposure systems, *everyone* should carry a camera, and I mean by that, actually take the camera along while hunting.

Though I use a full *system* 35mm reflex camera for much of my work, with various lenses and accessories, my hunting camera that rides in my pack is a high-grade range-finder camera with its normal 50mm lens. This is a light and compact camera and takes up little room in my pack. The only accessories carried are one or two filters and a lens hood. Photos made with this simple equipment have appeared in various national magazines, some as covers, and the editors neither knew nor cared what camera was used to make them.

My point here is that a complicated, bulky, and expensive camera need not be used in order to get good pictures. There are now on the market some fine medium-priced cameras with excellent lenses and automatic exposure systems. These cameras are small enough to fit in a pocket, and, if carried in the pack, they take up less room than an extra box call. By all means load the camera with color film of the type that produces positive transparencies, such as Kodachrome or the faster Ektachrome. These transparencies can be projected in all their brilliant color on a screen, and, if wanted, black-and-white or color prints can be made from them.

10

Woods, Navigation, and Travel

TURKEY HUNTING will at times entail travel and movement through large wilderness areas, especially when hunting in our national forests such as the Monongahela in West Virginia and the Francis Marion in South Carolina, both of which offer excellent turkey hunting opportunities. Some state forests also cover vast expanses of wild and woolly terrain.

Let it be stated as an article of faith that no hunter should ever enter any extensive forested area at any time without having in his possession a good reliable compass *and* the knowledge of how to use it. Some men pride themselves on possessing a "sense of direction." I wouldn't bet on it! I've had some spooky experiences while traveling in the company of some of these self-proclaimed "experts."

What many hunters do have is a good and almost instinctive habit of being aware of their surroundings at all times. A good habit to cultivate, by the way. As they travel through any unfamiliar territory, these men will without conscious effort be constantly checking the lay of the land, outstanding physical features, drainage of water, direction of the sun if it is visible, prevailing wind direction, and how their back trail looks in relation to outstanding landmarks. They will also have a well-developed sense of *travel time.*

All this has an important bearing on the ability to traverse unknown country, but sometimes natural phenomena such as fog, blizzards, and storms can change the picture drastically. An instance of this occurred some years ago when I was hunting deer in territory so familiar to me that I knew certain trees and glacial boulders on sight. They were like old friends.

On this particular morning a dense fog had descended over my hunting grounds. Vision was limited to a distance of about ten feet, but I had no qualms about entering this block of woods that was bounded on four sides by roads forming a square approximately three miles to a side. I decided to head straight in from the road, traveling due north until I reached a stream that flowed from east to west. I would then follow the stream in a westerly direction for about one and one half hours, hunting along the way, and then travel due south back to the road from which I had started.

All went well until I reached the stream. Instead of flowing from the right—east—it was flowing in the opposite direction. I was puzzled momentarily—this was the only stream that flowed through this block of woods—until I pulled out my compass. Instead of facing north as I should have been when I reached the stream, I was now facing south. Having faith in my compass and traveling south as it indicated, I reached the road on which my car was parked and ate my lunch, meanwhile puzzled as to how I had crossed the stream in the fog and come upon it from the north.

By now the sun had emerged and burned away the fog. I reentered the woods and soon had the answer to the puzzle. Following my morning's tracks in the light snow that covered the ground, I discovered that I had unknowingly crossed the stream at a point where a great flat rock spanned the water, forming a natural bridge. I had then circled left in the fog and arrived at the stream on its north bank.

To add to my chagrin, there, only thirty feet downstream, was a huge hemlock that I knew well, but had been unable to see in the dense fog. I relate this incident only to illustrate how fog, storms, and other natural happenings can alter our conception of place and direction even in country we know well. Had I been checking my compass as I should have done due to the fog, I would not have experienced the queer feeling I had when I discovered the stream flowing in the "wrong" direction.

Some men are extremely sheepish about consulting their compass in the presence of others, apparently feeling that such an action marks them as being somehow less "woodsy" than their companions. The same fellows have no compunction about glancing at their watches for information as to the time of day. The compass is a fascinating little instrument and should be consulted often by all who roam the far sides of the mountains and the valleys between.

Merely looking at his compass and determining which way lies north is of little practical use to the woods traveler. The compass has much more confidential information to impart if we will only seek its advice. By use of the compass alone, no maps, the hunter can wander at will in territory bounded by easily recognized roads, streams, hills, and other natural boundaries. This may be all that is required of the compass under the particular circumstances. This was my sole use of the compass—when I had sense enough to use it—on the occasion just related when dense fog obscured landmarks in territory that was totally familiar to me.

A second use of the compass is the following of a line from "here" to "there," technically called "following a bearing." The hunter may top out on a high ridge from which he can see a lake, open field, fire tower, or other landmark. He wishes to go from where he is located, which may be unknown, to the fire tower, which he knows has a service road connecting to the road on which his car is parked.

He orients his compass by turning it so that the north end of the needle points to the north marking on the dial. Keeping the compass oriented, he sights across the dial toward the fire tower and reads the degree marking that coincides with the direction in which the tower lies. Let's say the reading is 60 degrees. By finding a tall tree, prominent rock formation, or other easily seen object that lies in that direction, he puts his compass away and walks directly toward the object. On arriving at the rock formation, he finds that the fire tower is now hidden from view because he has descended a slope and tall trees block his direct line of vision to the tower. Again orienting his compass, he sights another landmark that lies in the direction he wishes to travel—60 degrees—and travels in as straight a line as possible toward this second landmark. Repeating the process with successive landmarks, each on a bearing of 60 degrees from each other, he will eventually arrive at or near the fire tower.

Any deviation from the direct line of travel such as would be necessary if the hunter arrived at an impassable bog, pond, or other barrier, which would require him to walk around it, should be compensated for by taking a compass bearing at each turn and consulting the watch for travel time on each new bearing.

As an example—the hunter, traveling on his bearing of 60 degrees toward the fire tower, arrives at the shore of a pond. He travels along the shore of the pond on a bearing of 150 degrees for ten minutes, at which time he arrives at the end of the pond and can pass around it. He now travels for ten minutes on a bearing of 330 degrees, which should bring him to a point just about opposite to the point where he first came upon the pond. He then resumes travel on a bearing of 60 degrees as before.

A third use of the compass sans map is the ease with which it allows the hunter to return directly to his car, camp, or other location situated on a road, stream, or long lakeshore that cuts through his hunting grounds. Before entering the woods from such a fixed boundary, orient the compass while facing in the direction you will be traveling. Let's again say that you find this bearing to be 60 degrees. Jot this down so that you do not forget it. Now, before starting out, determine the direction of your "back-bearing," which will be your return direction when your hunt is over for the day.

Do this by adding 180 degrees—the number of degrees in a half circle —to your direction of travel, 60 degrees. Your back-bearing will be 240 degrees and you'll find it directly opposite 60 degrees on your compass dial. Jot it down. If you should find that the bearing on which you will start out is *greater* than 180 degrees, *subtract* 180 degrees to find your back-bearing. Example—the direction in which you will enter the woods is 280 degrees. Subtract 180 degrees. Your back-bearing is 100 degrees.

This use of the compass is especially simple if your entrance into the woods is up the side of a steep ridge that parallels the road or trail from which you will start out. I sometimes take both my direction of entrance and my back-bearing in the late afternoon or early evening of the day before if my hunt will start before daylight. This is especially useful when I have located a turkey gobbling on his roost in the evening. I arrive at my starting point next morning, check my entrance bearing, and start right out.

There is nothing complicated about these simple uses of the compass,

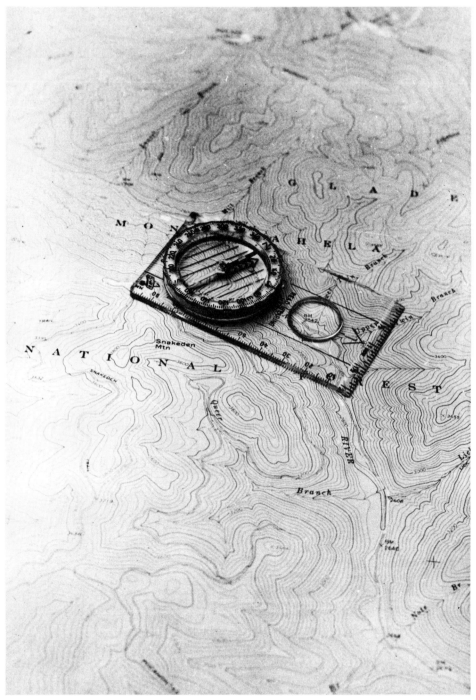

Topographic maps and a good compass are essential to the hunter who traverses wilderness hunting grounds. The modern Silva orienteering compass shown here is versatile and easy to use.

though they may seem so on first reading. Take your compass out right now and review the foregoing. In a few minutes everything will fall right into place. Like anything else worth doing, practice in the use of the compass will lead to proficiency in its use.

The use of map and compass together greatly expands the usefulness of both to the woods traveler. For instance, I have on many occasions laid out my direction of travel and my back-bearing for my first day's hunt of the turkey season in new territory weeks in advance and while at home hundreds of miles from my proposed hunting grounds.

Good maps are not only an aid in navigating unknown territory, but are useful in laying out the hunt. Maps will also be found useful for locating likely turkey range.

There is no magic in this feat—I'm not a surveyor or engineer—just the application of plain common sense, good maps, and a good compass, and some exceptionally fine instruction material. For the latter I can highly recommend the book *Be Expert with Map and Compass* by Bjorn Kjellstrom. This book is available from many sporting-goods outlets or from the distributor, Silva, Inc., Highway 39 North, La Porte, Indiana 46350; it comes with a practice compass, protractor, and section from a topographic map. It is an investment worth far more than its modest price to all who will travel in the wilderness.

The use of the compass in all applications important to the turkey hunter is greatly simplified by the use of a Silva System "Orienteering" compass. This type of compass will enable you to determine your direction of travel directly without having to read and think degrees. Nor is it necessary when using these instruments to keep track of degrees by jotting them down or depending on your memory. Your return direction—back-bearing—is indicated automatically, with no necessity of adding or subtracting with the possibility of error that might cost you miles of unnecessary travel, or a night huddled over a fire in the woods.

They are unequaled for use in conjunction with maps. As an example of the usefulness of this type of compass when used with a map, consider the following. During last year's spring gobbler season in New York, I decided to hunt a steep ridge that paralleled a road. I had seen a gobbler cross this road on the previous afternoon during a heavy rain and proceed up the ridge.

The climb to the ridgetop from the point where I had sighted the turkey was precipitous and rough, as determined from a topographic map of the area. Further examination of the map disclosed a point where the road crossed a part of the ridge about a mile distant. If I started the hunt from this second point, I would be able to spend more time in hunting rather than just climbing. I could reach the point where I estimated the turkey to be by hunting along the ridgetop in the same amount of time that it would take me to climb to it from the road. Sitting at the table in my cabin, I was able to lay out an easy route on the map with all bearings determined beforehand.

The next morning, long before daylight, I parked my car, glanced at the direction-of-travel arrow on the Silva compass that I had set the evening before, and was enabled to have a pleasant morning's hunt with little climbing. I did not get the turkey. This was the bird mentioned in a previous chapter, the one that lifted straight off the ground like a woodcock and flew off through the trees.

Good maps are indispensable to any woods wanderer. The best of these are the topographic maps published by the U.S. Geological Survey. These maps cover all of the United States, and are available with scales of one inch equals approximately one mile on the 15-minute series, and one equals 2,000 feet or 666.6 yards on the 7½-minute series.

The 7½-minute series is by far the most useful to the turkey hunter. Details of terrain are easily discernible on the 7½-minute maps, but unfortunately they are not yet published for all areas in every state. Maps covering states east of the Mississippi River may be obtained by writing to the Geological Survey, Map Distribution Section, Washington, D.C. 20242. For areas west of the Mississippi River, write to the Geological Survey, Map Distribution Section, Federal Center, Denver, Colorado 80225. The first step in obtaining maps of your hunting territory should be a request to either of the distribution sections for an "Index to Topographic Maps" of the state in which you will be hunting. These are free for the asking.

These indexes are maps of the entire state, divided into "quadrangles." Each quadrangle is a map of a particular area, usually named for some prominent feature in the area, such as a mountain, large lake, or town. These quadrangles are the maps you will be using, and as mentioned before, they are obtainable in either 15-minute or 7½-minute series.

Study the index and determine which quadrangles cover the area of your proposed hunt. Ordering instructions are given in the index. Place your order well in advance of the beginning of your hunt, and when they arrive, study them closely. The amount of information that can be gathered about unknown territory from these maps is amazing.

Topographic maps will tell you much about the physical features of the area in which you will be hunting long before you arrive on the scene. They will indicate whether or not the climb from any given point to the top of a ridge will entail a stiff climb or an easy jaunt. Natural obstacles to travel such as bogs, swamps, rivers, and cliffs, and the best way around them, are easily determined. The natural boundaries of your hunting area will be indicated. Knowledge of these boundaries is particularly important if, despite all precautions, you should become lost. They are known features that lie in known directions, and, as a last resort, following a compass bearing directly to the nearest boundary will get you out of the woods or to some point in the area from which the way out can be easily determined.

In addition to the topographic maps, the turkey hunter will find that maps published by the U.S. Forest Service are very useful when hunting on national forest land. These maps can be obtained from the U.S. Forest Service, Washington, D.C. 20250. Maps are published for each of the national forests, and show features such as forest service facilities, trail and road numbers, etc.

Various state agencies publish maps covering state forests, parks, and public hunting areas. Some excellent turkey hunting can be found on many of these areas. Many of these maps contain symbols indicating what species of game are present on the various areas covered.

The smart turkey hunter will acquire a good compass and learn to use it with the dexterity and ease that will enable him to travel in wild country at will and with an easy mind. Combined with accurate maps such as the topographic quadrangles, and practice in using them together, his compass will add much to the enjoyment and successful conclusion of the hunt.

11

The Hunter

HAVING DISCUSSED THE WILD TURKEY, his habits and habitat, his quirks and foibles, his weaknesses and strengths, let's take a look at his adversary—you, the hunter.

The one thing that the turkey hunter can bring into the woods with him that will do the most to ensure the successful pursuit of this giant among game birds is a *positive mental attitude*. Such an attitude is more important than the best of calls and the finest of guns. Without it, all else is mere paraphernalia and window dressing. If it is lacking, the odds against the hunter are almost insurmountable.

Dependence upon "luck" is a common attitude among hunters of many game species. The question, "What luck?" is almost a cliché among them. Though happenchance does play a very minor role in hunting the wild turkey, he who depends upon it as his mainstay is doomed to spend fruitless hours, days, and even years before taking his first turkey.

This is particularly true when the quarry is that "egghead" among turkeys, *Meleagris gallopavo silvestris,* the eastern woodland turkey. Not that the other races of turkeys are easy marks for any hunter—far from it! But old *silvestris* is generally recognized as the smartest and wariest bird of them all, and the one most likely to give the hunter fits. I've often thought after one of this race had made a complete fool of me that his name should be changed to *Meleagris gallopavo intelligensis.*

If you are serious about your turkey hunting, forget "luck" and get to work. You'll find it to be the most pleasant work you have ever undertaken. You have placed yourself in good turkey country, scouted the woods for signs, and in the springtime have located several gobbling birds. You have already eliminated nine tenths of the luck factor by taking positive action.

I believe that most successful hunters—and anglers too—practice a form of self-hypnosis. These men just *know* that their efforts will be crowned with success. To them, it is the expected and normal result of their efforts afield. That this may not be so on any particular day does not discourage them in the least. Tomorrow will surely be the day. They know that game is using the area, and that their equipment is in good order. What reason, then, to doubt success?

On the other hand, it has been my observation that many hunters who take to the field each year carry with them a completely negative attitude. These are the ones who are always back at camp or car first. On any given morning they will have spent all of two hours in the woods, covering no more than a half mile to a mile when fall hunting, and climbing a short distance up some ridge in the spring. On questioning, they will tell you that they saw or heard nothing, and that there are no turkeys in the area anyhow. This last, despite all evidence to the contrary.

Further questioning will reveal that these "hunters" entered the woods, traveled some five hundred yards, sat down on some stump or log, practiced on their turkey calls—something they should have done long before the season opened—became bored and probably consumed their lunches, and then wandered back to car or camp. If they have returned to a car, they can usually be found sleeping in the back seat long before noontime.

However, they do have one positive attitude. They are positive that if they had been hunting in any other area, they would surely have their turkey by now. These are the fellows who, if allowed to have their way, would spend the balance of the day traveling from place to place in order to "look them over." You will notice that if there is a diner, coffee shop, or restaurant in the area, this is the spot that will get the most "looking over."

The negative attitude can manifest itself in more subtle ways, even among those hunters who are willing and enthusiastic. This is particularly true in regard to newcomers to the sport of turkey hunting. They will rise in the early hours, gulp a hasty breakfast, and be off for the woods before anyone else. They will climb the highest ridge, hunt the roughest terrain, and penetrate the deepest swamp.

But if all this effort is not rewarded by instant success, they become discouraged. Discouragement leads to carelessness in their hunting. They will cease to look for signs of turkeys, and will not travel the few hundred yards required to look over some promising cove or point. The edges of ponds and water holes—a prime location for finding turkey tracks—if not in their direct line of travel, will be neglected. Their ears become less attuned to the sometimes distant yelping or gobbling of turkeys.

During a recent spring gobbler season, I was talking with a man who is a dedicated and extremely successful turkey hunter. I mentioned a new area of the state that was being opened to turkey hunting for the first time by the inauguration of a spring gobbler season, and speculated as to what the results would be. His reply was: "Well, they'll come in herds, full o' snap and ginger just like they did when we had our first season in this region. They'll go bargin' through the woods rattlin' them calls at a great rate every ten steps and down every hollow. Then, when they find it ain't all that easy, why, next season, only the real turkey hunters or those with the makin's of turkey hunters will be back." He was probably right.

Carelessness can also be brought on by the excitement felt by a new hunter when he first experiences the pure joy of having a turkey answer his calling. If it is a gobbler in the spring, he will tend to move in too close to the bird, thereby spooking it. Or, he will call too often, with the attendant danger of sounding a sour note due to his inexperience with the call.

Failure to take full advantage of whatever cover is available, and unnecessary movement while a turkey is approaching, is another careless habit of the tyro hunter. This is a fault that I must admit I was guilty of until I lost several opportunities as a result. The new hunter wants to *see* the approaching bird while it is still far out of range.

This leads to much peering and bobbing of the head above the concealing cover. After he has lost a few birds by these actions, the hunter learns to be content with what his ears tell him about the approach of his quarry. There is a certain satisfaction peculiar to turkey hunting in just listening to the calling of an approaching bird. The nearest experience to it would probably be hunting moose and elk by calling them.

Carelessness in delivering the shot is another prime reason for an empty-handed return to camp by the turkey hunter. In most instances this takes the form of shooting at too long a range by hunters armed with shotguns. Riflemen are rarely guilty of this fault because they are more apt to know exactly what the path of their bullet's flight will be from the muzzle to the target at all normal woods ranges.

The shotgun is a short-range weapon. If this one fact can be implanted indelibly in the hunter's mind, it will do much to reduce the stories of lost chances that fill the evening air of most turkey camps. Visualize thirty yards. Pace it off at every opportunity so that the picture is impressed on the mind and memory. Stretch it to thirty-five yards on occasion, but try to err on the short side when a turkey is before your gun.

Unlike upland gunners, turkey hunters seldom actually hunt in pairs or groups. The very nature of the game precludes it. Two hunters may enter the woods together, but they will separate and perhaps hunt different sides or ends of the same ridge providing there is no danger of one interfering with the other. Obviously, two men will make more commotion than will the lone hunter, and two will find it more difficult to conceal themselves in the same hiding place.

Men will talk, and two hunters together will more than likely be gabbing when they should be listening. It should be obvious by now that the turkey hunter depends on his hearing to a much greater extent than on his vision. The close companionship of Ole Smitty may be a great source of pleasure to you, but forgo it while actually hunting turkeys.

An exception to this lone-hunting rule will be made when one hunter is to do the calling while the other does the shooting. This sort of arrangement will sometimes be made when a hunter who is new to the game is unsure of his calling ability, or to fool a wily bird that repeatedly eluded a lone hunter.

The man who is to do the calling will conceal himself some fifty to seventy-five yards to the rear of the shooter. When all is ready, he will begin calling while the other man devotes his entire attention to sighting the turkey and not moving so much as an eyeball until it is time to shoot. The turkey, his attention riveted on the source of the calling, is not so likely to spot the concealed front man. This trick will sometimes bring to bag a turkey who has time and again fooled a succession of hunters.

A variation of this tactic can be used on a turkey that has shown a predilection for circling the source of the calling. In this case the caller locates himself to the front of the shooter, who is concealed to the rear and to one side. When the turkey makes his circle, he will most likely come within range of the concealed shooter. Under these circumstances the shooter must be careful not to shoot in the direction of the caller.

What to do when entering the spring woods and meeting a strange hunter obviously intent on a gobbler you have both previously located? Personally, I would propose a toss of the coin to determine which of us is to work on his lordship on this particular morning. Two hunters trying for the same bird, while it might make for an interesting calling contest, will probably result in no turkey for either.

If, on the other hand, you hear another hunter working a bird before you start calling, and the turkey is obviously responding, it would be extremely poor sportsmanship on your part to horn in on the party. It is to be hoped that you have at least one other gobbler located. Go get him, and leave the other man to his sport.

I recall an instance when another "hunter" spoiled a morning's hunt for me during a recent gobbler season. I had located a gobbler the evening before and was on hand before daybreak the next morning to greet him. The turkey gobbled on his roost several times, and after a decent interval during which I was sure he had flown down, I sounded a series of soft hen yelps. The gobbler responded immediately, and we carried on an interesting conversation during the course of which he kept coming closer to my position.

When the turkey was within about fifty yards of me, I heard an unearthly screaming coming from somewhere below me on the ridge, coupled with a loud crashing of leaves and brush. The turkey continued to gobble when I gave forth another series of hen yelps. The screaming notes from below continued, and presently there hove into view a hunter clad in a white sweat shirt and electric-blue baseball cap. This lad was really dressed for the occasion!

As the newcomer paused momentarily, the mystery of the strange and bone-chilling sounds I had heard was solved. They were coming forth from the mouth of the stranger, as with a contorted face he attempted to use a diaphragm call that presently popped from his mouth and landed in the leaves at his feet.

As he bent over to retrieve the call, I was sorely tempted, but managed to control myself. Meanwhile, the gobbler had retreated up the ridge, gobbling intermittently on the way. I let go with a loud series of yelps on my box call to get the attention of my unmusical friend in the white sweat shirt, but he obviously could not make out my camouflaged form and continued to perform on the diaphragm call. His efforts produced notes such as I imagine would attend the despoliation of an owl.

As I continued to call, it finally dawned on Dinny the Dunce that there was another hunter on the ridge. His reaction was an amusing but obnoxious display of pique as he raised his gun and fired a shot up the ridge in the direction of the gobbler who was now a good two hundred yards away. If he couldn't have that turkey—a most unlikely event —nobody else could have him either.

This incident throws light on the inherent danger present when a hunter who is calling might be mistaken for a turkey by some such ignoramus as the lad in the foregoing tale. If you see another hunter in the area, by all means let him know of your presence.

This brings up another matter that I think should be clarified. There is a feeling among the personnel of some game departments that perhaps rifles should be barred for turkey hunting in the interest of safety. Their well-intentioned but somewhat fuzzy thinking is that a rifle bullet will do more serious damage than a charge of shot in the event of an accident.

The fly in the ointment is the fact that statistics show that most hunting accidents happen at short range—and are usually self-inflicted. At the short ranges at which most accidents occur, the shotgun is a fearsome weapon indeed. The likelihood of a shot pellet or bullet hitting a man decreases rapidly as the range increases, even by such small increments as fifty feet. In the case of the shotgun there are more individual missiles and therefore more likelihood of a hit. That's the whole idea of the shotgun in the first place.

A factor that must be taken into account is the fact that those hunters who prefer the rifle for turkeys are usually highly skilled shots who know the trajectory and range of their guns intimately and take great pride in *precision* shooting. Their rifles are for the most part equipped with telescope sights, which in themselves offer a margin of safety.

In the unlikely event that a rifleman should aim his gun in the direction of a concealed hunter under the impression that his concealed target is a turkey, his mistake will be readily apparent to the probing eye of his telescope sight with its ability to penetrate concealing cover and reveal things for what they actually are.

So, rather than prohibiting rifles for use in turkey hunting for reasons of supposed safety, it would make more sense to require their use—with telescope sights—and bar the shotgun. Preferring as I do to use the shotgun for most of my turkey hunting, I sincerely hope this never comes to pass.

I've heard some turkey hunters belittle the rifle as being unsporting when used for turkey hunting. This is a narrow-minded point of view. The rifleman's sport is derived from making a clean, precise kill at fairly long range. The shotgunner prefers to lure the bird in close where it can be taken with a charge of shot. Who is so arrogant as to say that one method is more sporting than the other? We seem ever ready to knock the other fellow's sport when our efforts would be more profitably spent in improving the opportunities for all to enjoy.

So far as the actual danger involved in hunting is concerned, all this is academic. Statistics from the major insurance companies, who take a cool, dollar-and-cents attitude toward such matters, show that you are in greater danger of losing your life or suffering grave injury while in your home, swimming, golfing, fishing, skiing, or engaging in a multitude of other activities, than you are while enjoying the sport of hunting. The greatest danger to hunters is while they are driving on the highways to their hunting grounds. Hunting is one of the safest of all sports.

Hunting the wild turkey sometimes involves travel and movement in extremely rugged and rough terrain. In some regions the hunter will face a stiff climb before he arrives in the area actually being used by turkeys. His physical condition may be the deciding factor between success and failure, between an enjoyable experience and a time of misery and frustration.

I had to learn the hard way. My first—and unsuccessful—turkey hunt was an expedition for spring gobblers in the mountains of West Virginia. I had laid on some winter fat and allowed my muscles to soften up after the previous fall's deer hunts. Except for the first morning, I did no really hard climbing, but was in no shape at all until the week's end. This poor physical condition slowed me up, and I did not cover half as much country as I should have.

Long before the next spring seasons rolled around, I started to toughen up my foot and leg muscles. I began by taking long walks in the vicinity of my home, and then hiking and climbing in the hill country about ten miles distant where I do most of my deer hunting. This regimen paid off in a much more comfortable time during the following seasons when I hunted in three states. I advise all who hunt to do likewise before taking to the woods.

This preseason conditioning need not be strenuous, but should be done on a scheduled basis. The idea is to tone up the muscles of your

Jim Brady holds a North Carolina gobbler.

legs and feet, and to increase lung capacity and circulation. Jogging is a fine way to accomplish these objectives, but is really more than is necessary if you are in any shape at all. If you are overweight, start peeling it off long before your hunt is to begin.

Though climbing will be the most strenuous activity engaged in by the turkey hunter, he will walk five miles for every mile climbed. In rolling country climbing is not a factor at all. Walk at every opportunity, and do it at a brisk pace; just sauntering along will do nothing for you physically.

I previously wrote at some length about the importance of a hunter's attitude in relation to the successful conclusion of the hunt. Attitude has another facet that bears on the hunter's total enjoyment of his sport. This can best be described as "The Happy Hunter—Harvest or None."

All of us who hunt do so with the prime objective of reducing the game to possession, otherwise it would be a pointless activity. The greatest experience in hunting lies in finally, after much travail, bringing our prize to earth. But I believe that those moments and hours and days between the start of the hunt and its ultimate conclusion are just as important to our enjoyment of the sport as is the final moment.

Who but the hunter ever really *experiences* daybreak? The casual hiker and camper in the forest may *see* daybreak, but only the hunter *feels* it. His whole mind, body, and spirit are alert and attuned to every slightest shift in the morning wind, to the faintest of bird notes, to the ticking sound of a falling leaf, and the changing, shifting shapes of the forest as the still-hidden sun begins its ascent.

Some of my most enjoyable hunting trips have been those during which I took no game. I've enjoyed the many—most—times when the wily turkey has won the contest. This is the feature about turkey hunting that keeps me coming back each season with an ever-growing enthusiasm. After he has gained some experience, during most seasons the turkey hunter will have birds answering and coming in to his calling. Whether he bags his bird or not, he will have enjoyed one of the greatest thrills that the sport of hunting has to offer. He will be the happy hunter —harvest or none.

12

Future Prospects

THERE IS NO POSSIBLE DOUBT about it. The response of the wild turkey to the changing character of millions of acres of our forest lands and to modern management techniques is the brightest star to appear on the horizon of game management and restoration in this century. Not since the introduction of the ring-necked pheasant—now declining in numbers—and the population explosion of the whitetail deer, both of which events began in the last century, has there been such reason to rejoice among sportsmen and other lovers of wildlife.

That this is merely the beginning of the story is a conjecture based upon fairly substantial evidence. Knowledgeable wildlife managers conclude that the turkey will continue to increase in numbers and to occupy new ranges as the habitat becomes suitable. In addition, there now exist millions of acres of prime turkey range that merely awaits the arrival of transplanted wild stock in order to become, in a few years' time, not only first-class turkey hunting territory but an additional source of brood stock to be used in stocking still other areas.

As important as the changes in forest habitat and the development of live-trapping and transplanting techniques are to the success and well-being of the wild turkey, other factors have been, and will continue to be, essential elements in the overall picture. Among these are a public attitude that will ensure the survival of brood stock in newly populated areas. It is an open secret among turkey management personnel in some areas that one of the greatest detriments to successful establishment of new populations is the poaching that begins almost as soon as the first turkey is sighted.

The wild turkey is a large, tempting, and desirable game bird, and some uncaring and selfish individuals who think of nothing but the satisfaction of the moment are unfortunately present in almost every community. Better law enforcement and changing attitudes are reducing the prevalence of poaching, but it is still a factor to be reckoned with.

More of an irritant than anything else is the selfish and proprietary attitude that comes to the fore among some so-called sportsmen and others in areas with well-established turkey populations, when livetrapping operations are conducted in order to obtain birds for transplanting into other prime turkey range. They object to the removal of a small portion of "their" birds, conveniently forgetting that "their" birds are descendants of turkeys that were trapped elsewhere and released in their home territory.

The question of their greediness aside, what these folks fail to understand is that with each successful establishment of a huntable population elsewhere, the hunting pressure on their home grounds is reduced. I've been told by one wildlife technician that the sight of his truck with its prominent departmental insignia cruising the back country is enough to set the wires to the state capitol afire. Such an attitude is inexcusable. Here again, better education of the public is the answer.

I've detected some grumblings of late among grouse hunting purists who are concerned with what to them is the unseemly maturation of large areas of forest land. They decry the disappearance of old and well-loved grouse coverts, swallowed up by the natural process of forest growth. I can truly sympathize with them, having conducted a life-long love affair with old *Bonasa umbellus,* the ruffed grouse. But I've flushed many a grouse while hunting turkeys, and I have many times listened to the drumming of grouse on the slopes below me while hunting gobblers in the spring.

In order to get some expert opinion on this seeming grouse-turkey conflict—or to determine if it really existed—I asked Wayne Bailey for his projection on the future of turkey hunting. Wayne spent some twenty years with the West Virginia Department of Natural Resources, where he worked on both grouse and wild turkey projects before moving to North Carolina.

I don't believe Wayne has yet decided which he loves most between turkey and grouse hunting, and so has sensibly decided to settle down and enjoy the pursuit of both these splendid American game birds. His answer to my query follows.

Regarding your question on possible grouse-turkey conflicts: They can, of course, coexist as occurs throughout Virginia, West Virginia, and Pennsylvania. I would think, however, that to manage any large area exclusively for either species would be of extreme detriment to the other. The greater the number of stems to the acre, the better the habitat for grouse; contrary-wise, extensive, open understories provide the most optimum range for turkeys. It is, of course, *diversity* of tree species and age classes that permit both to occupy the same general area.

Today, the system of silviculture referred to as "Even Aged Management" (EAM), which, essentially, is clear-cutting, is in vogue. Where the objective is the production of *sawtimber* on a sustained yield basis (that is, clear-cutting small blocks on a long-term rotation cycle), the needs of both grouse and turkeys will be met fairly well, but conditions for neither will be optimum. Where the objective is the production of pulp, the balance will tip in favor of grouse, as the rotation cycle will not be long enough for good turkey range to develop. The fact that both species are plentiful in West Virginia means that over any large area we can have good hunting for both.

Regarding the future of turkey hunting: For the country as a whole, I think there is going to be a continuing steady improvement for quite some time due to the fact that so much good range remains to be occupied. We are also learning quite a bit more about how to manage land for turkeys and how to better handle turkeys themselves. Even more important, the recent upsurge in interest in spring gobbler hunting means that we can now extract from the species the maximum in recreational benefits *without harm to the species.*

On the negative side, the continued increase in human populations and the subsequent demands on the land and all its resources, particularly its tree resources, will inevitably constrict the space and habitat needed by the turkey. The ultimate fate

A message from the Forest Service designed to acquaint the public with the "blessings" of clear-cutting. Despite this awkward attempt at public relations, the real reason for promoting clear-cutting is the fact that it is the cheapest method of timber harvest.

of the turkey will, in my opinion, impinge largely on human population trend.

The above are, I know, sketchy answers to some very big questions. If you pursue the subjects at length, a longtime but interesting job awaits you. Let me know if I can help—or confuse—further.

As can be deduced from Wayne's letter, with proper management of our forest lands, both grouse and turkeys can continue to provide excellent hunting far into the foreseeable future with but little conflict between the two species. However, professional foresters are unfortunately afflicted with a tunnel-vision that allows them to see a forest as being primarily for the production of timber, with but little attention given to other considerations such as esthetic values and recreation.

Values other than timber production are given a perfunctory nod with little positive action taken or even contemplated. I make this statement principally in regard to our publicly owned national forests. The only positive action is that which generates the veritable blizzard of propaganda booklets and brochures that fill my mailbox to overflowing.

I have before me as I write a publication received from the National Forest Products Association that is designed to acquaint the public with the "blessings" of clear-cutting. Other screeds of like ilk have been received from the United States Forest Service, produced and mailed, of course, at public expense. This agency is charged with managing our national forests for the benefit of the people of the United States as a whole, with all values to receive equal consideration.

At times, one gets the distinct impression that the Forest Service sees itself as the mouthpiece for the timber industry. There seems to be the same *buddy-buddy* atmosphere here that is sometimes apparent between the Federal Power Commission, the Atomic Energy Commission, aided and abetted by the Corps of Engineers, and the power industry that these agencies are supposed to regulate.

I have seen the glories of clear-cutting firsthand. On a spring day several years ago I hunted a section of the Monongahela National Forest in West Virginia, which was at the time beautiful turkey range, and on

The approach to a clear-cut area is one fraught with the feeling that a great desecration has been done. The feeling of death is in the air.

which we called up three gobblers. I should have been forewarned of coming disaster when I discovered a giant beech tree fully four feet in diameter, girdled around its entire circumference in such a way as to ensure its death. On inquiry, I was informed that this was the work of the Forest Service, who considered this to be a "wolf tree," which was shading out the—to them—more desirable softwoods.

I revisited the area during this year's spring season in anticipation of some fine sport, and was greeted with a scene of utter desolation. Every tree had been cut down, with not a stick left standing. Dead tree-tops and slash were everywhere, and the beginnings of erosion were clearly evident. My partner, Dr. Virgil Polley, on his first turkey hunt, gazed on the scene in shocked silence.

We were standing in a biological desert. No sign or sound of bird, animal, or even insect could be seen or heard. To add insult to our wounded spirits, there stood a sign, courtesy of the United States Forest Service, extolling the benefits of clear-cutting to mankind.

The alleged benefits of clear-cutting accrue only to the timber industry. This is the cheapest method of harvesting timber. You can bet your Afghan rug that this is the only reason why it is practiced and put

Once beautiful turkey range on the Monongahela National Forest has been clear cut, this area will not again harbor turkeys during the lifetime of any adult now living.

A growing number of sportsmen have come to consider the wild turkey as being the greatest trophy available to the hunters of America.

forward as being environmentally desirable by the timber marauders and their lackeys.

If clear-cutting were limited to small areas of some twenty-five acres or less, not much harm would be done so long as large areas remained with trees in various stages of growth, and the trees along watercourses and slopes subject to erosion were left standing. This system of timber harvest would provide habitat in which nut-bearing trees would remain, along with fruit-bearing understory plants.

Long sawtimber rotation and harvesting by selective cutting and thinning encourage stands of mixed trees. In fact, such cuttings increase mast production and the survival of hardwoods, both of which are vital to the welfare of the wild turkey.

I hold with the philosophy that private property is to be used by the owners—within certain constitutional limits—as they see fit. But public lands such as our national forests are held in trust for all the people, and are not the private domain of the lumberman, the miner, or the cattle-man. They are not only *our* forests, but also *our* trees! This last fact is one which the despoilers would like to ignore—and will if we let them get away with it.

On the bright side, good turkey habitat is probably increasing at a faster rate than the chain saw is chewing it up. A good word here for the Forest Service. The modern forest fire control techniques that have been developed by the service have saved untold millions of acres of prime forest lands from the devastation of that greatest *clear-cutter* of all, wild-fire. So far as hunting is concerned, under present regulations governing the sport, turkeys are more likely to be under-harvested than over-harvested. The hunter in territory far beyond the ancestral home of the wild turkey, notably in Washington, Oregon, and California, has been given the opportunity to hear the reverberating gobble of The Mountain Shaker.

The story of the return of the wild turkey has all the drama and color of a fine and successful theatrical production. As in all such productions, a prime requisite to success is, in the language of the theatre, the pres-ence of an *angel,* he who provides the financial support that makes the whole thing possible.

The angels in this story are the sportsmen, the hunters, who, through their license fees and the taxes paid on their equipment under the pro-visions of the Pittman-Robertson Act, have provided the millions upon millions of dollars needed for game research and management.

The sportsmen of America occupy a rather unique position in that they requested that these fees and taxes be imposed upon them. Through their efforts alone during the last three quarters of a century, the welfare of the wildlife of the nation, which includes more nongame than game species, has prospered.

It is only fitting, therefore, that this book should close with a salute to those first and most dedicated ecologists and environmentalists, those who have, in the vernacular, "put their money where their mouths are." They have, indeed, put their money where their hearts are.

Firms manufacturing and dealing in turkey hunting equipment and calls

BURNHAM BROTHERS, P.O. Box 92, Marble Falls, Texas 78654. Calls, camouflage equipment.

GANDER MOUNTAIN, INC., P.O. Box 248, Wilmot, Wisconsin 53192. Calls, camouflage equipment.

M. L. LYNCH COMPANY, P.O. Box 377, Liberty, Mississippi 39645. Manufacturer of box- and slate-type turkey calls. Instructions.

P. S. OLT COMPANY, Pekin, Illinois. Manufacturer of calls.

PARKER DISTRIBUTORS, 40 Industrial Place, New Rochelle, N.Y. 10805. Calls, camouflage equipment.

PENN'S WOODS PRODUCTS, INC., 19 West Pittsburgh Street, Delmont, Pennsylvania 15626. Manufacturer of five types of turkey calls and specialized equipment for the turkey hunter.

Selected Bibliography

AMERICAN ORNITHOLOGISTS UNION
Checklist of North American Birds. A.O.U., 1957.

BAILEY, R. W., and RINELL, K. T.
History and Management of The Wild Turkey in West Virginia. West Virginia Department of Natural Resources, 1968.

DAVIS, H. E.
The American Wild Turkey. Small-Arms Technical Publishing Co., 1949.

EDMINSTER, F. C.
American Game Birds of Field and Forest. Scribners, 1954.

HEWITT, O. H. (ed).
The Wild Turkey and Its Management. The Wildlife Society, 1967.

LATHAM, R. M.
The Complete Book of The Wild Turkey. Stackpole, 1956.

McILHENNY.
The Wild Turkey and Its Hunting. Doubleday-Page, 1914.

PLIS, S., and HARTMAN, G.
Are the Turkeys Talking? Wisconsin Conservation Department, 1968.

SCHORGER, A. W.
The Wild Turkey: Its History and Domestication. University of Oklahoma Press, 1966.

THOMAS, J. W., and GREEN, H. W.
Something to Gobble About. Texas Game and Fish Commission, 1958.

TURPIN, TOM.
Hunting the Wild Turkey. Penn's Woods Products, 1966.

WISSLER, C.
The American Indian. Oxford University Press, 1938.

INDEX

M

Maps, 134
    sources of, 134, 135
mating yelp, 83
Mexico, 12

N

nesting, 25
net, mortar-thrown, 17

O

Ontario, 12
"owling," 48, 50

P

pack, hunting, 122
Penn's Woods Products, 83
physical conditioning, 143
predation, 30
pulmonic puff, 52

R

races, of turkeys, 23
raingear, 118
rifles
    cartridges, 106
    rifle-shotguns, 103
    use of, 142, 143
Rocky Mountains, 12, 18
roosting, 70

S

scouting, preseason, 46
scratching, 35–37
shotguns

action types, 89
barrel length, 98
barrel regulation, 92
choke devices, 93
gauges for turkey hunting, 92
Ithaca Model 37, 90, 98
patterning, 93
shot sizes for, 96, 98
weight, 100
social order, of turkeys, 27
South Carolina, 13
spring hunting, biological basis for, 46
strutting, 25

T

telescope sights, 106, 109
ticks, 124
tracks, 73
travel (by turkeys), 38

V

vision, of turkeys, 53, 71